# BIG, NOT SO EASY: COMPARING INSURGENCY THEORY TO THE COMPLEX PROBLEM OF VIOLENCE IN NEW ORLEANS

Pages Intentionaly left Blank

Pages Intentionaly left Blank

Pages Intentionaly left Blank

# ABSTRACT

BIG, NOT EASY: COMPARING INSURGENCY THEORY TO THE COMPLEX PROBLEM OF VIOLENCE IN NEW ORLEANS, by Major Dwight D. Domengeaux, Jr., US Army, 65 pages.

This research proposes that violent gangs are similar to insurgent cells in their organization and their methods of gaining control of an area or population. Recognizing that insurgent organizations and gangs are complex adaptive systems, this monograph uses Jamshid Gharajedagi's context, structure, function, and process analytical model to compare the two phenomena. The monograph will use New Orleans, Louisiana as a case study to illustrate the similarities between gangs and insurgents, and, to examine the efficacy of a counterinsurgency approach to addressing the gang problem.

The hypothesis for this monograph is that some aspects of counterinsurgency theory and doctrine are applicable to combating violent gangs in New Orleans. To develop the argument in support of the hypothesis, the research will seek to answer the following research questions: Do violent gangs in New Orleans, resemble insurgent cells, if so, in what ways? What aspects of counterinsurgency theory or doctrine apply to countering violent gangs? What changes in doctrine, organization or technology will help New Orleans' law enforcement and its government in countering gang violence in its neighborhoods? To answer the research questions, this study will include literature reviews and data analysis from the academic fields of political science, criminology, sociology, and history. The research concludes by recommending an operational approach that will aid the City of New Orleans and its Police Department in combating violent neighborhood gangs.

# ACKNOWLEDGMENTS

This research is inspired by the lives of Chester J. Reeder, III and Napoleon Washington. This work would not have been possible without the support that I have received from a loving family. Joan, Lauren, Catherine, and Olivia, every paragraph within this monograph represents time spent away from you, thank you all for the understanding and the help. I owe a great deal of thanks to Ms. Sarah L. Schirmer of the New Orleans Innovation Delivery Team for her advice, research assistance, and for working to help New Orleans reach its full potential. Dr. Cox and COL DeTingo, thanks for allowing me to choose a topic that is a slight departure from the norm, and for leading me through the process. Finally, I would like to thank the library staff of the Combined Arms Research Library (CARL), your daily assistance and pleasant customer service contributed immensely to this monograph.

# TABLE OF CONTENTS

# ACRONYMS

| | |
|---|---|
| ADM | Army Design Methodology |
| BJA | Bureau of Justice Assistance |
| COIN | Counterinsurgency |
| DoJ | Department of Justice |
| FBI | Federal Bureau of Investigation |
| MAG | Multi-Agency Gang Unit |
| NATO | North Atlantic Treaty Organization |
| NOLA | New Orleans, Louisiana |
| NOPD | New Orleans Police Department |
| OCGS | Organized Crime and Gang Section |
| OEF | Operation Enduring Freedom |
| OIF | Operation Iraqi Freedom |
| RICO | Racketeer Influenced Corrupt Organization |

ILLUSTRATIONS

TABLES

# INTRODUCTION

Today, however, we have to say that a state is a human community that (successfully) claims the monopoly of the legitimate use of physical force within a given territory. Note that 'territory' is one of the characteristics of the state. Specifically, at the present time, the right to use physical force is ascribed to other institutions or to individuals only to the extent to which the state permits it. The state is considered the sole source of the 'right' to use violence.

—Max Weber

The renowned German philosopher Max Weber argued that the social institution known as the state would not exist were it not for the use of violence. Weber asserts, "force, (violence), is a means specific to the state."[1] The authority to use violence implies that a state can deliberately inflict harm on its people to achieve a legitimate end.[2] In modern western societies, citizens confer upon the state the authority to use violence by complying with socially accepted behavioral norms, and thru adherence to formal legal codes.[3] The state's use of violence is functional, in that states use violence with the intent of preserving social order. Violence is legitimate only when necessary to secure the state's institutions and protect its citizens.[4] Illegitimate violence, conversely, is violence used within the state's territorial boundaries to disrupt social order and to challenge the state's legitimate control of the territory. Insurgents and criminal gangs, inherently, challenge the state's monopoly on using violence. In some circumstances, insurgencies, and or, gangs possess the organizational and material strength to subvert the state's sovereignty, and to undermine the state's legitimate control within its territory.

---

[1] H. H. Gerth and C. Wright Mills, "Politics as Vocation," in *Max Weber: Essays in Sociology* (New York: Oxford University Press, 1946), 77–128, http://www.sscnet.ucla.edu/polisci/ethos/Weber-vocation.pdf (accessed December, 29, 2013).

[2] Stathis N. Kalyvas, *The Logic Of Violence in Civil War* (New York: Cambridge University Press, 2006), 19.

[3] Gerth and Mills, "Politics as Vocation," 2.

[4] Kalyvas, *The Logic Of Violence in Civil War,* 19.

Criminal gangs, and the members that make up their ranks, are analogous, in many ways, to insurgent organizations. Insurgents and criminal gangs are social phenomena, and as such, one should view them as complex systems.[5] This monograph will analyze insurgents and criminal gangs within the environmental context that each of these phenomena develop. The environmental context in which an insurgency is likely to occur is an unstable area with underlying civil tensions. Insurgencies emerge out of unresolved conflicts between opposing sides. In general, the government (incumbent) seeks to maintain the status quo and the insurgent aims to change the existing order. There are myriad of destabilizing factors (real and perceived) existing within the environment that, potentially, laid the foundations of an insurgency—including ethnic oppression, widespread poverty, and socio-political injustice. Likewise, street gangs thrive in areas that are rife with underlying social, economic and, in many cases, ethnic tensions.[6]

Gangs and insurgents organize using similar structures. A clear similarity between the gang and an insurgency is the comparable demographic groups that fill the ranks of both. Insurgencies and gangs recruit from similar pools of potential fighters, disenfranchised young men unsatisfied with their lot in life. Roger Trinquier's description of insurgent recruiting in 1960s Algeria is useful in illustrating some of the similarities between gang members and insurgent cell members. Trinquier asserts that, "the foot soldiers are recruited from the

---

[5]Mary Jo Hatch and Ann L. Cunliffe, *Organization Theory* (New York: Oxford University Press, 2006), 331.

[6]Max G. Manwaring, *Street Gangs: The New Urban Insurgency* (Carlisle, PA: U.S. Army War College, 2005), 5; Anthony James Joes, *The History and Politics of Counter Insurgency* (Lexington, KY: The University Press of Kentucky, 2004), 24.

impoverished areas of the city, from the population of delinquents or habitual criminals."[7] Insurgent cell members join the insurgency because they are discouraged and angered by the policies and perceived illegitimacy of the existing government or civil authority. Similarly, gang theory suggests that individuals migrate towards sub-cultures such as a gang to express their dissatisfaction and frustration with their perceived inability to achieve success, given the existing social norms. In turn, the individuals blame the system and join a gang to "wage war" against the society, that they believe to be unjustly holding them back.[8] Gangs and insurgents self-organize into a decentralized network of operatives, each with a function related to the political cause, in the case of an insurgency, and a criminal enterprise in the case of the gang. Both organizations, gangs and insurgents, serve several functions: to further their specific enterprise (whether political or criminal), to protect the organization's members, and to defend their territory.

The undeniable aim for both insurgencies and gangs is to win control, or if control is already established, maintain control of the population, while at the same time denying control to the government. Gangs and insurgents conduct their specific functions, criminal and political, within the territory that they control. Gangs or insurgents are sometimes able to operate freely, without the fear of denouncement. This is so because of their relationship with the local population; a relationship often based on social bonds and familial ties.

The primary means used to gain control and accomplish their respective functions is violence. Insurgents and street gangs both use violence as a process for gaining control within a

---

[7]Roger Trinquier, *Modern Warfare: A French View of Counterinsurgency* (London: Pall Mall Press, 1961).

[8]Jane Wood and Emma Alleyne, "Street Gang Theory and Research: Where Are We Now and Where Do We Go from Here?" *Aggression and Violent Behavior*, no. 15 (2010): 101–11.

3

geographic area.[9] Insurgencies use terrorism and guerilla tactics, whereas street gangs commit murder as violent means to control and coerce the population.[10] Insurgents and street gangs employ a process of violence to intimidate the population into collaborating, or at least tacitly supporting the insurgent's subversive activity or gang's criminal enterprise. In addition to coercing the population's support, insurgents and gangs use violence to punish their rivals, discredit the law enforcement, and to encourage popular denouncement of the local government authorities.

## The Problem

For many years New Orleans, Louisiana has been, statistically, one of the United States' most violent cities. On a number of occasions, New Orleans' annual homicide totals earned the city the dubious title of "murder capital of America." Although the entire city is affected negatively, violent crime, specifically homicides, are concentrated in a small number of New Orleans' neighborhoods. Areas of New Orleans that, historically, account for the excessive number of homicides are the same areas of the city plagued by neighborhood gangs operating the retail drug market.[11] The areas of New Orleans accounting for the majority of the homicides also have characteristics of social disorganization. Structural problems such as high unemployment,

---

[9]Kalyvas, *The Logic of Violence in Civil War*, 21. Kalyvas distinguishes between violence as an outcome and violence as a process. The author argues that nonviolent actions that precede and follow violence are often linked.

[10]John Simerman, "New Orleans Taliban Gang Targeted in State," *The Advocate: New Orleans Edition*, 18 August 2013, http://theadvocate.com/news/neworleans/6785061-148/new-orleans-taliban-gang-targeted (accessed December 29, 2013).

[11]Ibid.

low educational levels, separated families and under-performing social institutions, especially schools, create ideal conditions for the emergence of neighborhood street gangs.[12]

In neighborhoods controlled by street gangs, citizens sometimes do not denounce the gangs or their illicit activities, because they are fearful for their own safety or because they are generally distrustful of the local government. The trust deficit and lack of faith between the population and the local authorities causes citizens, in some neighborhoods, not to collaborate with law enforcement. The absence of collaboration deprives the police of the very information required to reduce crime and bring security to the neighborhood. When citizens refuse to collaborate with the police, the result is a reinforcing feedback loop that accelerates the growth in homicides.[13]

Limited collaboration between the population and the government equates to increased street gang control. This monograph asserts that criminal gangs are responsible for the statistically high rates of murder in New Orleans. Criminal gangs use a process of violence to establish control of their neighborhood's territory, and to protect their criminal enterprise.[14] The aim of this research is to analyze the similarities of criminal gangs and insurgent organizations. If the research findings indicate that significant similarities exist in the structure, function and processes of insurgents and gangs, then it is reasonable that counterinsurgency theory and

---

[12]Barbara D. Warner, Elizabeth Beck, and Mary L. Ohmer, "Linking Informal Social Control and Restorative Justice: Moving Social Disorganization Theory beyond Community Policing," *Contemporary Justice Review* 13, no. 4 (December 2010): 355–369.

[13]Peter M. Senge, *The Fifth Discipline: The Art and Practice of the Learning Organization* (New York: Doubleday, 2006), 79. Reinforcing feedback effects occur when a small change builds upon itself, for example, the movement of a snowball rolling downhill is amplified with each subsequent movement, the snowball moves faster and grows larger.

[14]Ibid, 21.

doctrine offers methods applicable to New Orleans in its effort to combat criminal gangs and violent crime.

## Methodology

This research proposes that violent gangs in New Orleans, Louisiana are similar to insurgent cells in their organization and their methods of gaining control of an area or population. The monograph will use New Orleans as a case study to illustrate the similarities and to examine the efficacy of a counterinsurgency approach to addressing the gang problem. The working hypothesis for this monograph is that aspects of counterinsurgency theory and doctrine are applicable to combating violent gangs in New Orleans. To develop the argument in support of the hypothesis, the research will seek to answer the following research questions: Do violent gangs in New Orleans, resemble insurgent cells, if so, in what ways? What aspects of counterinsurgency theory or doctrine apply to countering violent gangs? What changes in doctrine, organization or technology will help New Orleans' law enforcement and its government in countering gang violence in its neighborhoods? To answer the research questions, this study will include literature reviews and data analysis from the academic fields of political science, criminology, sociology, and history. The study will also draw on the body of military knowledge associated with insurgency and counterinsurgency theory.

The monograph focuses on twentieth century (primarily post World War II) insurgency theory as the basis of the research because of its current contextual applicability. For example, David Galula's *Bourgeois Nationalist* Pattern of insurgency is instructive in drawing similarities between an insurgent network and street gang's operational approach to establishing a base of operations.[15] To establish a model of comparison between gangs and insurgencies the monograph will draw from classic literature and gang research especially the seminal research conducted by Fredric M. Thrasher and the conception of social disorganization and gang formation popularized by Clifford Shaw and Henry McKay of the University of Chicago's School of Sociology.[16]

Insurgents and gangs often operate at a material disadvantage in comparison to their government opponents. In order to overcome their material disadvantage, insurgents, and street gangs, must be able to live and hide within their own territory. Gaining control of the population is the way that insurgent organizations and neighborhood gangs are able to survive and prolong their conflict against the counterinsurgent or local law enforcement agencies. Conversely, the local government and law enforcement (counterinsurgents) must gain (or regain) the trust and active support of the population in order to be recognized as the legitimate authority.

In addition to social disorganization theory, Chapter two of this research will also introduce political science professor Dr. Stathis Kalyvas' concept of zones of control. Kalyvas' description of zones of control is useful as a method to analyze how belligerents establish control within a contested area.[17] The case study will describe the City of New Orleans spatially in terms of Kalyvas' zones of control. Using zones of control as a model will allow the author to reduce the contiguous area of New Orleans into separate parts. The analysis will focus on the interstitial areas of the city that account for most of the violence attributed to gangs, specifically murders.

This study asserts that street gangs share certain characteristics with insurgent cells. It is therefore necessary to analyze the literature on insurgencies and gangs separately and then

---

[15]David Galula, *Counterinsurgency Warfare: Theory and Practice* (St. Petersburg, FL: Hailer Publishing, 2005), 58.

[16]Dr. George W. Knox, *An Introduction to Gangs*, 6th ed. (Chicago, IL: New Chicago School Press, 2006), 147.

[17]Kalyvas, *The Logic of Violence in Civil War*.

summarize the similarities. The monograph will analyze modern insurgency theories to determine how insurgents use context, structure, function, and processes used to exert control over a population.[18] The monograph will take the same approach to examine the formation and activities of street gangs. The intent here is not to equate all insurgencies to gangs, nor is this study intending to draw parallels between a specific insurgent cell and a specific gang in New Orleans. However, this study will synthesize the literature, examine the similarities and compare the general characteristics of the two phenomena.

The research hypothesis asserts that counterinsurgency theory is applicable to combatting violent street gangs. Specifically, this monograph will analyze population-centric counterinsurgency methods that have proven effective for the US Military and coalition forces during Operation Iraqi Freedom (OIF) and Operation Enduring Freedom (OEF). The research will conclude by recommending an operational approach that will aid the City of New Orleans and its Police Department in combating violent neighborhood gangs.

<u>Study Limitations</u>

Time and resources limit the scope of this research to using the city of New Orleans as a single case study. The author acknowledges that the amount of violence (murders in particular) and the causes of violence differ from city to city and over time as conditions and resources change. However, the author contends that using New Orleans, as a single case study is adequate because that city has been plagued, for many years, by exorbitantly high rates of violent crime.

---

[18]Jamshid Gharajedagi, *Systems Thinking Managing Chaos and Complexity*, 2nd ed. (New York: Elsevier Inc, 2006), 110. Dr. Gharajedagi advocates the context structure, function and process framework to gain holistic understanding of a complex system. Structure defines components and their relationships; function defines the outcomes or results produced; process defines the sequence of activities and context describes the environment in which the system operates.

Therefore, the chosen case study will provide ample source information to answer the research questions and to test the hypothesis.

Historians, political scientists and military practitioners alike are aware that there are many varied reasons that insurgencies emerge. It is also true that the insurgent's social or political cause is, sometimes, more legitimate, internationally, than the existing government regime. For the purposes of this monograph, the researcher assumes that the government and its security forces (incumbents) are in fact the legitimate authority and that they do not represent an illegitimate and repressive regime. Therefore, the reader should assume that insurgents and gangs, in the case of this monograph, are subversive, illegitimate, and illegal actors.

This research contends that insurgents and gangs use similar violent methods to intimidate, coerce, and influence the population into supporting their causes. To make this comparison it is necessary for the author to equate the insurgent's socio-political cause to the street gang's cause. The insurgent organization's goal is to overthrow the existing political order by use of force. Research indicates that the objective of street gangs, particularly those that operate in New Orleans is primarily financial gain related to criminal enterprise (illegal drug trade for example).[19] The differences in purpose of the two organizations will assuredly necessitate some differences in methods and organization. However, the author contends that enough similarities exist to support the research hypothesis. This research includes analysis of scholarly literature, crime trend data, and socio-economic statistics to aid in developing an understanding of the current environment, (high murder and gang violence in New Orleans). The researcher also conducted interviews with city officials and law enforcement to gain an understanding of the desired future conditions-low murder and low gang violence.

_____

[19]Edward Evans and James Spies, "Insurgency in the Hood: Understanding Insurgencies Through Urban Gangs" (Master's thesis, Naval Postgraduate School, 2006), 3.

# LITERATURE REVIEW

Social disorganization theory, popularized by Clifford R. Shaw and Henry D. McKay, argues that widespread poverty and social instability in urban poor neighborhoods correlates directly to gang development and the spread of crime. Social disorganization occurs when a community is unable to achieve shared values, and when there is a breakdown in community institutions such as churches, schools, and most importantly families.[20] Disorganization intensifies in areas with structural deficiencies such as, high rates of unemployment, and low rates of educational achievement are concentrated in urban neighborhoods.[21]

Shaw and McKay asserted, "very often the child's access to the traditions and standards of our conventional culture are restricted to his formal contacts with the police, the school, and various social agencies." They go on to say, however, "[the] most vital and intimate social contacts are limited to the spontaneous and undirected neighborhood playgroups and gangs whose activities and standards of conduct may vary widely from those of his parents and the larger social order."[22]

Fredric M. Thrasher's conception of "gangland" noted that the gradual erosion of conventional social institutions and employment opportunities in urban areas contributed to social disorganization.[23] Disorganization in urban neighborhoods inhibits the practice of informal social control. Informal social control refers to the casual observation of neighborhood activities, or the direct intervention by concerned neighborhood citizens to disrupt inappropriate behavior and

---

[20]Wood and Alleyne, "Street Gang Theory and Research," 102.

[21]Warner, Beck, and Ohmer, "Linking Informal Social Control," 356.

[22]Knox, *An Introduction to Gangs*, 148.

[23]Wood and Alleyne, "Street Gang Theory and Research," 102.

delinquent activities.[24] The presence of informal social control in a neighborhood or village, on the other hand, presents the image of a cohesion within the area.[25] Disorganized neighborhoods with low levels of informal control are ideal context for the emergence of street gangs and insurgents. The existence of injustice, real or perceived, within the social-political-economic environment provides the, would-be, gang member or insurgent with a unifying cause to exploit.[26]

Violence, Collaboration, and Control

A very succint and unambigous definition of violence is offered by Stathis Kalyvas in *The Logic of Violence in Civil War.* Kalyvas states,"violence is the deliberate infliction of harm on people."[27] Insurgents and gangs use violence as an effective tool in pursuit of their similar goals of establishing territorial control and control within a population.[28] Violence, when used as a means to gain control of an area and compliance from a targeted population, is defined as coercive violence.[29] When used for coercive purposes, violence, in effect is a resource, a means to an end. Insurgents, use violence specifically in the form of terrorism aimed at non-combatants, and armed geurrilla combat, directed against the governments' security forces. Insurgents use violence to isolate the government from the population and to create a geographic demarcation between government authority and insurgent control.

---

[24]Warner, Beck, and Ohmer, "Linking Informal Social Control," 356.

[25]Ibid.

[26]"Social Disorganization Theory and Rural Communities," *OJJDP Bulletin*, May 2003, https://www.ncjrs.gov/html/ojjdp/193591/page1.html (accessed December 29, 2013)

[27]Kalyvas, *The Logic of Violence in Civil War,* 19.

[28]Ibid., 17.

[29]Ibid., 26.

Kalyvas contends that violence can be produced by either one actor or by competing actors. The significant difference is that in the case of competing actors such as (insurgents and the government) or (neighborhood gangs and the police) the population has an option to choose which of the rivals to support. Members of the contested population exercise their option by either withholding or sharing information with one of the opposing actors. They also have the option to provide material and moral support to the competing rivals (collaboration). The population's options, however, are influenced by coercive violence. Insurgent violence, therefore, is a tool to coerce the contested population into supporting the insurgents, or as a means to deter the population's collaboration with government security forces.

The support of the population comes in two forms according to Kalyvas, attitudinal support and behavioral support. Attitudinal support describes a relationship in which the population prefers to align with either the insurgent cells or the government forces. Although not measureable in a tangible sense, the side that gains the population's attitudinal support, the side preferred by the population, possesses an advantage in the contest for control.[30] Behavioral support is displayed when the population's support shifts beyond the intangible realm of attitudes and is translated into observable actions on behalf of one of the rivals. The population's behavioral support is evident in such actions as its willingness to provide information, recruits, and logistical support for the insurgents.

The population's compliance in, and acceptance of an abstract level of violence committed by the insurgents is yet another measure of behavioral support. However, using violence beyond the theoretical level deemed acceptible, such as indiscriminately killing citizens or murdering a beloved innocent figure within the community, can cause a previously supportive

---

[30]Ibid., 92.

population to denounce the actor that is responsible for the violence. When violence reaches such a level that the population chooses to denounce the insurgents, the insurgents risk a resultant shift in popular support. The population changes its behavior in favor of actively supporting and collaborating with the government.[31]

Michael Freeman argues that citizens in a community will accept a level of violence, between zero and (x) number of murders over an abstract time period before it demands that the government and the police department take significant action to reduce the violence. Freeman suggests that there is a gap between the accepted level of violence (x), and the actual level of violence (y). The terror gap indicated between (x) and (y) equals the amount of fear within the community. In other words, the terror gap (figure 1) is the difference between the actual level of violence and the amount of violence that the population is willing to accept before considering their village or community insecure (y-x = terror).[32]

---

[31]Ibid., 29-31.

[32]Michael Freeman and Hy Rothstein, *Gangs and Guerillas: Ideas from Counterinsurgency and Counterterrorism*, Defense analysis report (Monterey, CA: Naval Post-Graduate School, March 2011), 33 The figures were adapted from Micheal Freeman's literature on the "rationality of violence." Freeman used the graphic description to argue his views about what happens when people become desensitized to terrorist violence. I have adapted his and modified his charts to illustrate the potential effects that violence has on a local population.

Photo Removed Due to Copyright Restrictions

Figure 1. The Terror Gap

*Source*: Adapted from Michael Freeman's "Rationality of Violence" by the author.

Over time, if the police and government are ineffective in reducing the level of violence, Freeman theorizes that the population may become accustomed to the higher status quo of violence. The population's tolerance level for violence (x) will increase at least until it reaches the actual violence level (y). This phenomenon is alarming because it suggests that the population is uncertain of the government's competency and ability to protect them. In other words if the government cannot protect its population, its legitimacy is challenged and it begins to lose control within the local area. The government's loss of control will likely cause government collaborators within the the population to change their behavior, denounce the government, out of fear of insurgent reprisals. Paradoxically,when the population becomes accustomed to violence at a certain high level, the gap between (x) and (y) (the terror gap) will shrink.[33] Since we have earlier established that insurgents use violence as a means to coerce popular support, we can therefore argue that the shrinking terror gap (figure 2) is tantamount to a reduction in insurgent control.

---

[33]Ibid., 34.

14

Photo Removed Due to Copyright Restrictions

Figure 2. The Shrinking Terror Gap

*Source:* Adapted from Michael Freeman's "Rationality of Violence" by the author.

In order to prevent a marginal loss of control and to reestablish or widen the terror gap, insurgents may choose to increase the actual violence levied against the contested population. Freeman, however, suggests that there is a threshold of violence against the population that insurgent sympathizers will hold as sacrosanct, grapichally represented as (z). The variable (z) may be defined as an amount of violence, or it may represent an unacceptable type of violence, the murder of young children or a respected community leader for example.[34] However, as depicted in figure 3, once actual violence (y) exceeds the level of violence deemed acceptable by sympathizers (z), insurgent supporters will denounce the insurgents and begin to collaborate with the government.

---

[34]Ibid.

Photo Removed Due to Copyright Restrictions

Figure 3. The Violence Threshold

*Source:* Adapted from Michael Freeman's "Rationality of Violence" by the author.

Organized violence employed by an insurgent cell or a neighborhood gang is purposeful; the violence is intended to shape the behavior of the targeted victims and to communicate a message to the watchful population. Consider this example: an insurgent cell, or a gang, murders a police informant to stop him from collaborating with the police. Murdering the informant will not only deny the police access to specific information, the violence, also communicates to others that it is unsafe to turn against the insurgent or gang. The violence committed against an individual has wide reaching effects, it deters others within the contested population from collaborating with the government or police. In this case, violence perpetrated by the insurgents or gang has punitive and deterrent characteristics. There is a psychological or sociological argument to be made as to wheter or not violence is an effective punishment or behavioral deterrent, however that debate is outside the scope of this research. The point here is that coercive violence, is used by insurgents and neighborhood gangs to establish and exercise control of a geographical area and a specific population.[35]

Stathis Kalyvas argues, that competing actors in an insurgency (government or insurgent) will face three population sets: populations under the control of either side, populations that they must share, and populations that are completely outside of their control.[36] Kalyvas asserts that the actor exercising the higher level of control within an area will receive a greater degree of collaboration from the civilian population within that area.[37]

According to Kalyvas the fight for support of the population between the government, (incumbent), and the insurgent can be visualized as a competition over spatially divided sovereignty within the contested area.[38] Conceptually, and physically in some instances, the geography is divided into zones of control, ranging from total government control (zone one) to total insurgent control (zone five). In between the two extremes, lay the truly contested areas. Areas that are primarily dominated by the incumbent are labelled as zone two, whereas zone four are areas of dominate insurgent control. Zones of control three are areas that experience equal levels of control by the incumbents and insurgents, in other words there is parity of control.[39]

---

[35]Kalyvas, *The Logic Of Violence in Civil War*, 26-27. Kalyvas focuses on civil war and insurgent violence. The reference to gang violence is an inference made by the author based on gang violence literature that posits a similar theory to Kalyvas.

[36]Ibid.

[37]Ibid.

[38]Ibid., 88.

[39]Ibid., 196.

Photo Removed Due to Copyright Restrictions

Figure 4. Zones of Control Model

Source: Adapted from Stathis Kalyvas' *The Logic of Violence in Civil War,* created by the author.

The level of control reflects the probability of wheter a certain event, neighborhood gang violence in this case, will occur within a defined area.[40] This study uses Kalyvas' research regarding zones of control (figure 4) as a model to analyze New Orleans neighborhood gang patterns of violence. For the purposes of this study, New Orleans neighborhoods labelled as zone one represent areas in which the local citizens, city government, and law enforcement openly collaborate; the police have achieved complete control, and there are few gang homicides. Conversely, distinct parts of New Orleans experience a disproportionate amount of violent crime,

---

[40]Ibid., 210.

specifically homicide. These areas will be considered comparable to Kalyvas' zone of control five, insurgent control.[41] Zone five areas are those neighborhoods where gangs are capable of committing their violent acts, sometimes openly, with relative impunity. This is so because the neighborhood is controlled by the gang, the community fears repraisal, and they distrust the local authorities. Therefore, the populations in zone five neighboorhoods are less likely to openly collaborate with the city government, and law enforcement officials.

## Insurgents

No two insurgencies are alike, the nature of the conflict differs in each circumstance; one must first understand the nature of the type of war in which he is engaged.[42] It is outside the scope of this research to survey the many methods and varying causes of insurgencies. However, it is necessary to develop a general understanding of the nature of an insurgency in order to make an adequate comparison to neighborhood street gangs. This chapter will define insurgency and analyze the variables that are important to an insurgent organization using Jamshid Gharjedhagi's context, structure, function and process framework.[43] No singular insurgent approach is suitable to all socio-political contexts. Therefore, this monograph includes literature detailing a variety of insurgent approaches, specifically drawing on methods from urban and protracted popular insurgency approaches.[44]

---

[41]Ibid., 196.

[42]Mao Tse-Tung, *Selected Military Writings of Mao Tse-Tung* (Fort Leavenworth, KS: Combat Studies Institute, 1985).

[43]Gharjedagi, *Systems Thinking Managing Chaos and Complexity*, 108.

[44]Department of the Army, Field Manual (FM) 3-24.2, *Tactics in Counterinsurgency* (Washington, DC: Government Printing Office, 2009), 1-8.

## Context

United States military doctrine defines an insurgency as an organized movement aimed at the overthrow of a constituted government using subversion and armed conflict. Insurgencies are organized social phenomena that aim to weaken the established government's claims to legitimacy and control, while increasing the insurgency's control.[45] In essence, insurgents and their opponents, counterinsurgents (both internal and external), are fighting for control of the population.

Insurgencies have occurred in many forms within various socio-political, geographic and historical contexts throughout history. In scholarly literature, the term insurgency is synonymous with revolutionary war; as such, it is useful to propose a definition of revolutionary war. David Galula defines revolutionary war as an internal conflict wherein an organized group challenges the power of the controlling administration, police and armed forces.[46] Insurgencies and revolutionary wars have proven to be extremely adaptive to their environments. The original cause for the growth of an insurgency may scarcely continue to exist as the social context, and structure of the insurgent group changes.

Belligerents have waged insurgent conflicts for the purposes of combating ethnic and religious rivals, as a means of countering government oppression (real or perceived), and in resistance to colonialism and foreign invaders.[47] Early historical examples of insurgencies include revolutionary wars fought on two continents in the late eighteenth century. The Colonial Americans, especially in the southern colonies, fighting against British rule and French citizens

---

[45]Ibid., 1-1.

[46]Galula, *Counterinsurgency Warfare: Theory and Practice,* 3.

[47]Joes, *The History and Politics of Counter Insurgency,* 24.

revolting against the injustices of their monarchy. Early in the nineteenth century, Spanish guerrillas waged a bloody protracted insurgency that contributed to Napoleon Bonaparte's defeat in continental Europe, ironically, less than twenty years after the French Revolution.[48] Since the end of World War II, people's war, revolutionary wars, guerilla conflicts, small wars, low intensity conflicts, or whatever contemporary term used to describe the phenomena of insurgency, has been the predominate form of conflict in the world.[49]

Insurgency literature and historiography indicate that all insurgencies have in common an intent to subvert or overthrow the existing authorities.[50] Forced political change is the common, broad, purpose of disparate insurgencies. However, like all phenomena involving primarily human interactions, insurgencies are dynamic and complex.[51] The literature indicates there is not a single overarching cause responsible for all insurgent movements. However, scholarly literature overwhelmingly supports the claim that where insurgencies occur there are existing underlying tensions within the population. When manipulated by a determined individual or group (insurgents) the existing tensions transform into a unifying cause, or a call to arms that the population supports.

Insurgencies are very different in their specific root causes; sociological, psychological, cultural, political, and economic circumstances will all, in some way contribute to the formation of the insurgent ideology. However, Anthony James Joes argues there is often a single

---

[48]Department of the Army, Field Manual (FM) 3-24, *Counterinsurgency* (Washington, DC: Government Printing Office), 1-3; Joes, *The History and Politics of Counter Insurgency*, 2.

[49]Department of the Army, FM 3-24, 1-4.

[50]Ibid., 1–1; Trinquier, *Modern Warfare: A French View of Counterinsurgency*; Galula, *Counterinsurgency Warfare: Theory and Practice*; Frank Kitson, *Low Intensity Operations: Subversion, Insurgency, and Peacekeeping* (St Petersburg, FL: Hailer Publishing, 2006); Joes, *The History and Politics of Counter Insurgency*.

[51]Gharajedagi, *Systems Thinking Managing Chaos and Complexity*.

predominant factor that tips the balance of socio-political tensions from political unrest into the realm of insurgency.[52] Choosing a popular cause is an important first step in the insurgency's development. The best cause is one that a great proportion of the contested population supports.[53] The insurgency's leaders should identify with the chosen cause and endeavor to spread the ideology throughout the population for the purposes of creating an organizational identity, strengthening the insurgent support base, and increasing insurgent control. David Galula argues, "where there are no problems, there is no cause."[54] However, in the real world of constant interaction, between people and their environment, problems always occur. The insurgent cause forms out of recognition, opposition, and exploitation of, (real or perceived), socio-political, economic, racial, and religious problems.[55]

The existence of a popular cause is an indispensable requirement in the insurgent's quest for popular support. Support of the population in the words of Roger Trinquier is the *"sine qua non"* of victory in insurgent warfare. Any attempt to organize an insurgency without a popular cause is doomed to failure.[56] The importance of a unifying cause is evident in light of the proposed definition of an insurgency, as primarily a fight for legitimacy and control. If a popular cause does not exist or if it is not popular enough to influence the population over to the side of the insurgents, then, as Kitson suggests, the organizers of the insurgency must create a crisis. In

---

[52]Joes, *The History and Politics of Counter Insurgency*, 24. Joes argues insurgencies are often incited by a few specific elements: rigged or suppressed political elections, a tradition of internal conflict, a response from a segment targeted by genocide, the political or power aspirations of a marginalized group, and religious conflict.

[53]Galula, *Counterinsurgency Warfare: Theory and Practice*, 20.

[54]Ibid., 21

[55]Ibid., 22

[56]Kitson, *Low Intensity Operations: Subversion, Insurgency, and Peacekeeping*, 29.

this case, the insurgent leaders will manipulate a local grievance to construct a more popular cause.[57]

A counter-argument, against the need for a unifying popular cause within the contested area, is the "focoism" method of insurgency employed by Fidel Castro and Ernesto Che Guevara. In opposition to the idealism inherent in the protracted "people's war" waged primarily by communist insurgencies in the 20th century, focoism emphasizes the military actions of the insurgent or guerilla fighter early in the struggle. Guevara argued, "it is not necessary to wait until all conditions for making revolution exist; the insurrection can create them." In Guevara's view, the guerilla's violent attacks would create reinforcing feedback that would serve as the catalyst for expanding the revolution.[58] The primary objective, for the insurgents, was to demonstrate to the population the government's inability to protect its own forces and institutions from insurgent attacks. Guevara proposed that the population would support the insurgent's cause because of the successful attacks on the government. According to Guevara, the unifying socio-political cause was a secondary concern to gaining control through demonstrated military strength.[59]

Castro and Guevara were indeed successful in Cuba; however, it is arguable whether their success was a direct result of their methods. Because of existing socio-political injustices, the Cuban government at the time may have already been losing control of the population. Guevara's attempt to replicate the success achieved in Cuba, using the focoism model, met with disaster in

---

[57]Ibid.

[58]Senge, *The Fifth Discipline*, 79.

[59]Lt Col Sarah E. Zabel, "Military Strategy of Global Jihad" (Carlisle, PA: United States Army War College, 2007), 10.

Bolivia. Che Guevara paid with his life in Bolivia because his insurgency movement in that country did not develop a popular cause behind which the people rallied.[60]

The insurgent cause is of paramount importance, it is often to the insurgent's advantage to select more than one cause as the catalyst for conflict. Choosing a cause that is adaptable to the grievances of contested population is the optimal choice. The adaptability or opportunistic shifting of the cause implies that the pure ideology of the insurgent's cause is of subordinate importance to professing a cause that receives overwhelming support from the population that the insurgent is seeking to control.[61]

Structure

Social, political and economic conditions within a given geographic area or a specific population are the primary factors determining the organizational structure of the insurgency.[62] The seemingly unjust social conditions have stressful effects on the population; this creates tension and a sense of disaffectedness. An unjust socio-political environment, real or perceived, that seemingly gives favor to the political, religious, or ethnic group in power, contributes significantly to the disorganized social conditions in which an insurgency develops. A core group of proto-insurgent leaders and ideologists politicizes and exploit the perceived injustices, creating an environment ripe for gaining popular support and recruiting potential insurgent members.[63]

---

[60]Kitson, *Low Intensity Operations*; Zabel, "Military Strategy of Global Jihad," 10.

[61]Galula, *Counterinsurgency Warfare: Theory and Practice, 25.*

[62]Andrew Molnar, Jerry M. Tinker, and John D. LeNoir, *Human Factors Considerations of Undergrounds in Insurgencies*, U.S. Army Research (Washington, DC: Center for Research In Social Systems The American University, December 1966).

[63]Daniel Bynam, *Understanding Proto-Insurgencies*, RAND Counterinsurgency Study Paper 3 (Santa Monica, CA: RAND: National Defense Research Institute, 2007), vii. Insurgent movements start of as small bands of fighters with few members, little funding and limited

With a popular cause chosen, the insurgents now turn their focus to mobilizing the population, and building the insurgency's organizational structure. McCuen notes that mobilization "entails more than just winning the population over." Mobilization in the view of insurgent organizers includes person-to-person contact with the intent of intimidation, coercion, violence, and manipulation of information to "win" the populations support or compliance.[64]

By definition, the insurgents are at a great material disadvantage compared to the government authority that they aim to defeat. Other than having an ideal cause, the insurgents are without the necessary means to accomplish the political change that they seek. Because of this relative weakness, the insurgents are extremely vulnerable to the government's security forces.[65] The insurgent organization's growth, at this stage, depends heavily upon secrecy and the level of protection offered by the supportive population.[66]

While in its formative stages, ideally, the insurgency requires safe haven in a remote geographic area that is difficult to access and is outside of the government's control.[67] If such an area does not exist then another ideal location for the insurgents would be an urban population that is highly distrustful of the government's authority. The time horizon for an insurgency to spread its ideology throughout the selected area measures in months or years rather than weeks.

---

recognition or support, meanwhile the governments they oppose enjoy material and political advantage. Bynam argues that would-be insurgent groups must create, among other things, a relevant identity, and popular support.

[64]John J. McCuen, *The Art of Counter-Revolutionary War* (Harrisburg, PA: Stackpole Books, 1965), 54-55.

[65]Kitson, *Low Intensity Operations,* 32.

[66]Galula, *Counterinsurgency Warfare: Theory and Practice,* 29.

[67]Ibid., 39

This is true because the insurgency has to grow systematically if it hopes to establish a strong enough foundation to wrest control of the population away from the government.[68]

Galula offers two patterns for the emergence of insurgencies and the mobilization of the population. The *orthodox pattern* most often used by communist insurgents and the *bourgeois nationalist pattern,* which is a shortcut variation of the orthodox pattern. The orthodox method (table 1) in essence seeks to institute total political transformation. Its design includes five distinct steps that ultimately leads to the insurgents gaining total control of the country or contested population. This is the method used by Mao in China's revolutionary war.[69]

Table 1.    The Orthodox Method of Insurgency

Photo Removed Due to Copyright Restrictions

*Source:* David Galula, *Counterinsurgency Warfare*, table created by the author.

The Bourgeois Nationalist Pattern (table 2) is similar to the focoism theory used by Castro and Guevara in that this method uses violence by a small number of insurgents as the

---

[68]Kitson, *Low Intensity Operations,* 34.

[69]Galula, *Counterinsurgency Warfare: Theory and Practice,* 44-58.

means of coercing the population into denouncing the government and supporting the insurgency.[70] Unlike the Orthodox Pattern's goal of total political transformation, users of the Bourgeois-Nationalist Pattern primarily have a limited objective, to seize power and control of the population within the selected area.[71]

Table 2.    The Bourgeois-Nationalist Pattern of Insurgency

Photo Removed Due to Copyright Restrictions

*Source:* David Galula, *Counterinsurgency Warfare*, table created by the author.

Function

To have any success against their adversary, the insurgent group has to develop a support base within the contested population and develop an organizational structure that allows it to achieve success.  Insurgent organizational structures have taken various forms throughout history. The general structure, however, includes leadership, a mid-level cadre that focuses on politics, propaganda, weapons, logistics and other functions deemed necessary for the success and survival of the insurgency.[72]

---

[70]Ibid., 58.

[71]Ibid.

[72]Department of the Army, FM 3-24, 1-11.

A vital component to the insurgency's organizational development is the presence of a sanctuary or a safe base of operations. This sanctuary allows the insurgent group the time and space to recruit, train and equip themselves.[73] As noted, geography is an important factor in determining the insurgent group's development. Ideal locations for insurgent sanctuaries are isolated villages or neighborhoods surrounded by difficult terrain where government authority is weak or unrecognized. Other ideal locations for establishing insurgent sanctuary are those environments where the government shows little interest in the grievances of the population and the population perceives the government to be the cause of their discontent.[74] Within the isolated, disaffected populations, insurgent propaganda is often effective in influencing enough recruits to begin organizing into loosely ordered structures consisting of small cells.[75]

The basic cell consists of a leader that is a devoted full-time member of the insurgent organization. The leader in essence performs a supervisory role; he assigns tasks and ensures that the cell members are performing in accordance with established norms. The cell leader is also the link to higher echelons and the logistical support structure within the insurgency.[76] The intermediary serves as the cell leader's representative, or messenger, by delivering orders to subordinates and ensuring the timely flow of information back to the cell leader. Cell members perform tasks such as collecting money, distributing propaganda and carrying out violence or coercion on behalf of the organization.[77]

---

[73]Molnar, Tinker, and LeNoir, *Human Factors in Insurgencies,* 4.

[74]McCuen, *The Art of Counter-Revolutionary War,* 33.

[75]Molnar, Tinker, and LeNoir, *Human Factors in Insurgencies,* 5.

[76]Ibid., 6.

[77]Ibid., 7.

Figure 5 is an example of a small operational cell. The size of the cell varies depending upon the geographic area that it operates in and functions that it must accomplish. More importantly, the size of the cell depends on the level of security that the organization has within the population. A cell with limited support might well remain very small and compartmentalized, indicating sensitivity to a non-supportive environment, in order to protect its members, disguise its activities, and reduce the risks of capture.[78] Maintaining a small, compartmentalized cell allows the insurgent organization to "restrict the information any member has about the identity, background, or current residence of any other cell member."[79] In areas where the insurgents have established control over the population, and where it is less likely that government security forces can detect the cell's activities or infiltrate the organization, in zone five areas for example, insurgents use the operational cell model.[80]

---

[78]Ibid., 6.

[79]Ibid.

[80]Ibid.

Photo Removed Due to Copyright Restrictions

Figure 5. Operational Cell Diagram

*Source:* Adapted from Molnar, Tinker and LeNoir's *Human Factors Considerations of Undergrounds in Insurgency,* by: the author.

Cell leaders in a compartmentalized organization structure, represented in figure 6, rarely come into direct contact with the lower level cell members. The compartmentalized insurgent cell and similar cell types, place a premium on internal security; the cell design employs a system of indirect communication between members. Compartmentalized cells operate in areas where the insurgent group does not have control of the population. Rigid, compartmentalized cells are required in zone one areas, where the insurgents experience little or no freedom of action.[81]

---

[81]Ibid., 7.

Photo Removed Due to Copyright Restrictions

Figure 6. Compartmentalized Cell Diagram

*Source:* Adapted from Molnar, Tinker, and LeNoir's *Human Factors Considerations of Undergrounds in Insurgency,* by the author.

Process

Violence, particularly terrorism and guerilla attacks, is arguably the primary tool used by insurgents to advance their adopted cause.[82] Trinquier, writing about insurgencies in Indochina and Algeria, notes that the "basic weapon that allows a small weak insurgent to fight effectively against a regular army is terrorism."[83] Terrorist attacks, specifically against civilians within the targeted population, aim to instill fear, intimidate, and change the behavior and influence the decision making of the people.[84] The effects of terrorism on the population, however, go beyond

---

[82]Bynam, *Understanding Proto-Insurgencies,* 7.

[83]Trinquier, *Modern Warfare: A French View of Counterinsurgency,* 16.

[84]Fathali M. Moghaddam, "The Staircase to Terrorism," *American Psychologist* 60, no. 2 (March 2005): 161–69.

the suffering of the immediate victims. With an increasing amount of terrorism, a feeling of general insecurity permeates the contested area; the population begins to feel isolated and helpless. The population loses trust and confidence in the government, whose mission it is to secure them.[85] The ensuing loss of confidence in the government's ability to protect them causes some within the population to question the government's legitimacy; this, in effect, is a shift in attitudinal support.[86] Shifting popular attitudes contribute to a growing divide between the population and the government. The growing divide emboldens the insurgents, allowing them to operate with more freedom, and thereby increasing their control.

Increasing levels of insurgent control draws some of the contested population, either by defection or coercion, to the insurgent's side. The process continues as a reinforcing feedback system, gradually causing the population to denounce the government and to collaborate with the insurgents.[87] The shift in behavioral support signifies that the insurgent's process of violence has achieved its intended purpose, to win control of the population.[88] Using violence to control the population increases the insurgent's strength. Morally insurgents grow stronger because the population does not collaborate with the government, allowing more insurgent freedom of action. Insurgents are also stronger because they exploit their control of the population for material gain. Once insurgents gain control of the population within the geographic area, they are able to operate freely and establish a base of support from which to wage guerrilla warfare and directly attack the government's forces.[89]

---

[85]Trinquier, *Modern Warfare: A French View of Counterinsurgency*, 17.

[86]Kalyvas, *The Logic of Violence in Civil War*, 87.

[87]Senge, *The Fifth Discipline*, 79.

[88]Kalyvas, *The Logic of Violence in Civil War*, 87.

[89]Trinquier, *Modern Warfare: A French View of Counterinsurgency*, 19.

## Gangs

Scholarly literature from the criminology and sociology fields lacks consensus on a precise definition of what constitutes a gang.[90] As the statement "a gang of us went to the beach this weekend" suggests, gang is often used as an adjective to describe any group of people socializing, or working together. In fact American lawmakers commonly invoke a gang moniker when a bipartisan group bands together to solve the nation's problems, the "gang of six" for example.[91]

Using the term as merely a description for any group of people, undermines the serious threat that gangs pose to the many states, cities, and local communities that are plagued with gang violence. Therefore, it is necessary to define, in specific terms the meaning of the word gang as used in this monograph.

The United States Department of Justice (DoJ) has adopted the following definition of a violent gang: An association of three or more individuals; whose members collectively identify themselves by adopting a group identity which they use to create an atmosphere of fear or intimidation, frequently by employing one or more of the following: a common name, slogan, identifying sign, symbol, tattoo or other physical marking, style or color of clothing, hairstyle, hand sign, or graffiti. [92]

---

[90]Wood and Alleyne, "Street Gang Theory and Research," 101.

[91]Jeanne Sahadi, "What Gang of Six Plan Would Do," *CNN Money* (19 January 2011), http://money.cnn.com/2011/07/19/news/economy/gang_of_six_budget/ (accessed December 29, 2013). The Gang of six was a group of U.S. Senators working together to present a bipartisan budget plan focused on debt reduction, tax reform, reducing government spending, entitlement reform, and reform of the budget process.

[92]Department of Justice. "Department Of Justice: Organized Crime and Gang Section," Government Agency, *About Violent Gangs*, http://www.justice.gov/criminal/ocgs/gangs/. (Accessed 4 January 2014).

The DoJ expands its definition of gangs stating that the gang's purpose is "to engage in criminal activity and which uses violence or intimidation to further its criminal objectives with the intent to enhance or preserve the association's power, reputation, or economic resources."[93]

Gangs, according to the DoJ, particularly those gangs that are highly organized, possess all or some of the following characteristics:

1. The members may employ rules for joining and operating within the association.
2. The members may meet on a recurring basis.
3. The association may provide physical protection of its members from others.
4. The association may seek to exercise control over a particular geographic location or region, or it may simply defend its perceived interests against rivals.
5. The association may have an identifiable structure.

The Organized Crime and Gang Section (OCGS) of the DoJ broadly categorizes violent gangs into three types, street gangs, prison gangs, and motorcycle gangs. Specific references to gangs throughout the remainder of this monograph will narrowly focus on the DoJ's description and legal definition of a street gang.[94] This research does not intend to analyze trans-national gangs, international organized crime syndicates, or organized crime groups commonly referred to as La Cosa Nostra or the "mafia."[95]

---

[93]Ibid.

[94]Ibid. Street Gangs are located throughout the United States, and their memberships vary in number, racial and ethnic composition, and structure. Large national street gangs pose the greatest threat because they smuggle, produce, transport, and distribute large quantities of illicit drugs throughout the country and are extremely violent. Local street gangs in rural, suburban and urban areas pose a steadily increasing threat, transporting and distributing drugs within specific areas. The local street gangs often imitate the larger, more powerful national gangs in order to gain respect from their rivals.

[95]Ibid.

Context

In the United States, gangs have been a part of the American social construct for over 150 years. Gangs have varied thru the years in their reasons for being, ranging in purpose from political activists, to protectors of their respective ethnic groups. Gang sizes and types of organizational structure have also been dynamic features, constantly changing based on the given environment and the street gangs' chosen identities. Because their formation depends upon the existing social conditions, the moral sensibilities, character, and personalities of the individuals, no two gangs are exactly alike. However, the existing data show that the preponderance of street gangs display enough similarities to make the following generalizations. Young males, adolescent thru young adult, predominately ages (16-35), fill the ranks of street gangs. Gangs develop in urban areas experiencing higher than average poverty rates and unemployment, and lower than average education. The gang's primary purpose is protection of its territory, its members and criminal enterprise.[96]

Street gangs flourish in communities disconnected from the mainstream of the larger society within a given geographic area. The disconnected communities are typically poor, relative to other parts of the society at-large, and their neighborhood has decaying physical infrastructure. Fredric M. Thrasher uses the metaphor of "gangland" to describe these areas of a city.[97] Thrasher continues the metaphor by likening the city's center to a feudal kingdom with the accompanying

---

[96]Irving A. Spergel, *The Youth Gang Problem: A Community Approach* (New York: Oxford University Press, 1995), 56.

[97]Fredric M. Thrasher, *The Gang: A Study of 1,313 Gangs in Chicago* (Chicago, IL: University of Chicago Press, 1927), 6. As the title of the book indicates, the author conducted an extensive study of Chicago's gangs; however, his metaphorical description of Chicago's "gangland" is applicable to New Orleans, and arguably medium to large cities.

35

order and civil control. Gangland, however, lies outside the gates of the kingdom and the social boundaries of the mainstream civil society.

Disorder and violence are so prevalent in gangland that, to an outside observer, it may appear that the police and government have lost control.[98] Thrasher argues, "gangland represents a geographically and socially interstitial area in the city, in gangland there are breaks in the structure of social organization."[99] The presence of gangs is a characteristic of the comparatively unstable and disorganized areas of cities.

Gang literature and criminology research does not suggest that gang membership is a direct result of poverty. Nor, does it suggest that gangs exist only in urban areas and cities; there exists data to the contrary.[100] However, criminology and gang research indicates that there is a higher probability for gangs to take form in neighborhoods where, employment has diminished, there is poverty, deteriorating schools and dilapidated homes are common, and where citizens seeking more stability migrate to other areas of the city.[101] Geographic areas with such environmental characteristics as those described in Thrasher's "gangland" are ideal environments for the formation of a gang. The entire neighborhood, a particular block, or a specific street corner serve as potential breeding grounds for those groups of boys and young men that ultimately become gangs. Longtime childhood associations and familial ties form the nucleus of a neighborhood street gang. "In the more crowded sections of the city, the geographical basis of a

---

[98]Thrasher, *The Gang: A Study of 1,313 Gangs in Chicago,* 6.

[99]Ibid., 20. Thrasher used the term interstitial to convey that "gangland" was situated in the spaces between the mainstream of society, where fractured social-economic conditions resulted in collapsing social institutions.

[100]Spergel, *The Youth Gang Problem: A Community Approach,* 60.

[101]Thrasher, *The Gang: A Study of 1,313 Gangs in Chicago,* 20.

gang is both sides of the same street from a distance of two blocks.  The members are those boys who have played together; they know each other as well as brothers or sisters."[102]

## Structure

In their formative stage, new gangs evolve from spontaneous playgroups of boys from the neighborhood.[103] Individual boys or young men in the community may form a bond with like-minded members of the represented demographic. Once formed, the group assumes an identity based on a set of shared beliefs, grievances or a sense of dislocation. Based on the moral values, mental attributes and physical ability of the individuals, the emergent activities of the playgroup might range from athletic competition such as playground basketball to more illicit activities such as gambling or fighting against other groups.[104] Invariably, natural leaders emerge and the group leaders assign other members relative social standing within the group. As the group dynamics develop, and the frequency of interaction increases, the playgroup begins to evolve into a more organized hierarchical structure.[105] Thrasher's idea is that a playgroup, however, does not become a gang until it provokes opposition and disapproval from within the community or from rival groups.[106] The increased anti-social or delinquent behavior displayed, in response to perceived external threats, marks an important period for the group. The transition point from playgroup to gang occurs with the introduction of conflict; the group's response is to protect its members from

---

[102]Ibid., 25.

[103]Ibid., 23.

[104]Ibid., 26.

[105]Ibid.

[106]Ibid.

others (rival gangs, civil authorities, angry parents).[107] In response to rivalry, and opposition from outsiders, the playgroup draws closer together, and anti-social, delinquent behavior becomes the group norm.[108]

The group, then, begins to climb up the "staircase" toward an identity based on crime, and violence directed towards others in the community.[109] The essence of a gang, and what allows it to function, is the social bond that connects a group of boys or young men. The binding social connection is born out of a shared understanding or perception of the conditions existing within the group's environment. The disorganized environmental conditions existing within an area shapes an individual's behavior, his moral understanding and his general perceptions of distrust and anger towards the outside social world.

Constant interactions with individuals that share similar outlooks on life, lead the individuals to form a group that self-organizes and adapts to its environment. In the case of the gang, adaptation means organizing into a collective resistance against threats and providing a mechanism for its members to cope with the outside world.[110] Paradoxically, the gang's daily interaction within the community, and with other gang members, reinforces and accelerates the breakdown of legitimate social institutions within the gang's territory. The gang's criminal activities, violence, drug retail, and racketeering for example, shape the environment by creating conditions in which gangs continue to develop and thrive. The pattern of behavior demonstrated

---

[107]Ibid., 27.

[108]Wood and Alleyne, "Street Gang Theory and Research," 101.

[109]Moghaddam, "The Staircase to Terrorism."

[110]Everett Carl Dolman, *Pure Strategy: Power and Principle in the Space and Information Age* (New York: Frank Cass, 2005), 115.

in gang-community interaction illustrates a positive feedback system that perpetuates gang development.[111]

## Function

Neighborhood gangs thrive in, and control some areas because of social bonds and familial ties; the gangs are from the neighborhood. The gang members are in many cases the children, relatives and neighbors of the community residents. Establishing community ties is important because the gang needs the support and collaboration, voluntary or coerced, of the community in order to survive. Within the community, the gang finds a safe haven to shield its criminal activity from law enforcement. The community also provides a recruitment pool of young men and boys that can readily identify with the gang. The common identity eases the transition from delinquent youth to gang member. The community also provides information vital to the gang's security. The community's collaboration and information sharing provides early warning to the gang, and allows it to protect its enterprise against threats from the government, rivals, and denouncers.[112]

Max Manwaring identifies three generations of gangs, aptly, labeled as, first, second, and third generation gangs (table 3). First-generation gangs are small groups operating exclusively within a specific geographic area, or turf not more than a city block, or small neighborhood. First generation gangs commit low-level criminal activity; they are loosely organized cells, with a

---

[111]Senge, *The Fifth Discipline,* 79.

[112]James C. Howell, "Youth Gangs: An Overview," *Juvenile Justice Bulletin* (August 1998): 1–15.

decentralized leadership structure. The primary utility of violence for first generation gangs is to protect the gang's territorial integrity against threats from its rivals.[113]

The label second-generation gang implies a more centralized leadership and a somewhat sophisticated organizational structure. Whereas first generation gangs primarily conduct localized criminal activity, second generation gangs operate in wider, sometimes non-contiguous geographic areas. Second generation gangs use violence on a higher order than that of a first generation gang. Violence, for second-generation gangs, is a means of protecting the gang's criminal enterprise against competition, and to control the community in which they operate.[114]

Third generation gangs are those with expanded geographical parameters and highly sophisticated organizational structures.[115] Third generation gangs function as efficiently and effectively as major corporations. In addition to the specific criminal enterprise, third generation gangs implement a broad political agenda. They often possess the capability, and willingness, to use violence in direct attacks against the governing authorities and security forces within the gang's area of operation. In some countries, highly organized third generation gangs pose a very real threat to national sovereignty.[116]

---

[113]Manwaring, "Street Gangs: The New Urban Insurgency," 9.

[114]Ibid.

[115]Ibid., 10

[116]Douglas Farah, "Central America's Northern Triangle: A Time for Turmoil and Transitions," *PRISM* 4, no. 3 (2013). Transnational drug gangs are essentially threaten the sovereignty of some regions of Guatemala, Honduras, and El Salvador.

Table 3.    Generations of Gangs



Photo Removed Due to Copyright Restrictions



Source: Max Manwaring. "Street Gangs: The New Urban Insurgency," table created by the author.



## Process

Gang-related violence and violent crimes committed by gang members is disproportionately high when compared to crime data on non-gang members. To be sure, varying definitions and different legal classifications of what constitutes a gang member and gang-related violent crime increases the margin of error. However, the United States DoJ and Federal Bureau of Investigation (FBI) data attribute rising violent crime across the United States to gang activity.[117] Gang violence is a variable that increases or decreases depending on the given environment and level of support and control the gang has within its territory.[118] S. H. Decker argues that gang violence is a seven-step process, displayed as a cycle in figure 7.[119] Decker's process suggests that violence sanctioned by a gang, and committed by the gang's members relates to a specific purpose.  Decker's process also indicates that gangs target their intended

---

[117]Spergel, *The Youth Gang Problem: A Community Approach,* 33.

[118]Howell, "Youth Gangs: An Overview," 9.

[119]Ibid.

victims in response to, or in retaliation for some previous threat. Street gang violence, homicides in particular, are typically concentrated within certain areas of the city, and they involve disputes over territory, drug profits, or are in retaliation for some offense.[120]

Photo Removed Due to Copyright Restrictions

Figure 7. Seven-Step Violence Process

*Source:* Youth Gangs: an Overview Juvenile Justice Bulletin US Justice Department
Created by: the Author

The literature on gang violence indicates that gangs use violence purposefully to accomplish their goals and objectives. The popular culture portrayal of gang violence, particularly gang homicides, as indiscriminate acts is contrary to the data. To be sure, gang violence does cause unintended consequences, and innocent people are victims of gang related homicides. However, gang sanctioned homicides are committed to accomplish a specific purpose, or as a means to accomplish the gang's ends. According to data collected from nationwide police

---

[120]Ibid., 10.

districts, gang members are responsible for an average of forty-eight percent of the violent crime committed in the United States.[121] The DoJ attributes violent crime committed by street gangs to disputes over the retail drug markets, retaliation against a rival gang and enforcement of drug debts. The gang's purposeful and selective uses of violence, collectively, are measures taken to control the gang's territory.[122]

The *2011 National Gang Threat Assessment* notes, "gang membership continues to expand and form throughout communities nationwide. Consequently, gang-related crime and violence is increasing as gangs employ violence and intimidation to control their territory and illicit operations. Many gangs have advanced beyond their traditional role as local retail drug distributors in large cities to become more organized, adaptable, and influential in large-scale drug trafficking. Gang members are migrating from urban areas to suburban and rural communities to recruit new members, expand their drug distribution territories".[123]

Gang members also purposely use violence to intimidate and coerce non-gang members. In addition to the inadvertent or unintended consequence of violence enacted on innocents, "civilians" are sometimes the intentional targets of gang violence.[124] Overt and implicit intimidations are problems plaguing neighborhoods controlled by street gangs. Overt intimidation

---

[121]*National Gang Threat Assessment: Emerging Trends*, Federal Bureau of Investigation Report, accessed February 5, 2014, http://www.fbi.gov/stats-services/publications/2011-national-gang-threat-assessment/2011-national-gang-threat-assessment#CurrentGang (accessed February 5, 2014).

[122]James C. Howell, "Youth Gangs: An Overview."

[123]National Gang Intelligence Center, *2011 National Gang Threat Assessment – Emerging Trends*.

[124]Peter Finn and Jerry Murphy Healy, *Preventing Gang and Drug Related Witness Intimidation*, U.S. Department of Justice Report, Issues and Practice in Criminal Justice (Washington DC: National Institute of Justice, November 1996), http://babel.hathitrust.org/cgi/pt?id=purl.32754066627625;page=root;view=image; size=100;seq=3;num=i, 1 (accessed February 4, 2014).

is an explicit act designed to intimidate a citizen and influence his behavior. The direct threat of violence on a witness to the gang's criminal activity with intent to force the witness into withholding evidence or changing his testimony is an act of overt intimidation. Implicit intimidation, however, reveals an underlying community-wide climate of fear cultivated by gang control of the neighborhood and a history of violent retaliation. Brazen acts of criminal gang violence, such as a double homicide, committed in full view of spectators, serve multiple purposes, murder of the intended target, instilling fear into the community, and increasing the gang's level of control. Therefore, in light of the atmosphere of intimidation, the population's primary concern is for safety and individual survival. The public's perception that civil authorities cannot protect them reduces collaboration, and promotes a perception of non-cooperation with civil authorities.[125]

## Comparison Summary

Neighborhood gangs and insurgents are similar in context, structure, function and process. Review and analysis of insurgency and gang literature reveals that each phenomenon develops within similar social context. Insurgencies occur in social environments with underlying tensions such as ethnic oppression, widespread poverty, and socio-political injustice. Similarly, street gangs form and thrive in disorganized social environs, areas where poverty, poor education, and deteriorating social institutions are the norm.[126] Insurgencies and street gangs are complex social phenomena continuously adapting and providing reinforcing feedback to their environment. Insurgent violence for example, creates an atmosphere of fear and insecurity, which

---

[125]Ibid., 2.

[126]Manwaring, "Street Gangs: The New Urban Insurgency," 5; Joes, *The History and Politics of Counter Insurgency,* 24.

causes further destabilization of the social environment, thereby undermining the legitimate authority's control of the area.

Insurgents and gangs, alike, recruit adolescent males and young men from within these unstable environments. Some of the young male "recruits" willingly migrate towards sub-cultures such as a gang to express their dissatisfaction and frustration with their perceived inability to achieve success, given the existing social norms. They seek to belong to a group with a shared outlook, and together, they develop a group identity that forms the nucleus of the gang or insurgency. Often neighborhood gangs and insurgent cells intimidate and coerce the recruits into joining, or at least collaborating with the group. The key similarity however, is that neighborhood street gangs and insurgencies use violence as a means to challenge legitimate civil authorities for control of their respective territories and populations.[127]

The following anecdotal scenario illustrates the similarities in insurgent and gang processes. In order to establish control of their territory insurgents and gangs initiate a program of targeted violence. The purpose of the violence is to eliminate any perceived threat such as rival gangs, or different insurgent factions within the specified geographic area. After clearing the territory of direct threats, gangs and insurgents expand the process of violence (terrorism and murder) to establish control of the population in the area. They expand local control by actively targeting or threatening violence against civilian community and businesses leaders, ordinary citizens and infrastructure. The intent is to intimidate and coerce the population into actively supporting, or collaborating with the neighborhood gang, or insurgent.

Having succeeded in establishing control of the area, now, gangs and insurgents seek to secure and expand their influence in the area. From within the newly controlled area, insurgents

_____

[127]John P. Sullivan, "Future Conflict: Gangs and Intelligence," *Small Wars Journal*, 2009, smallwarsjournal.com, 1 (accessed February 4, 2014)

and gangs establish a network, of new recruits, informants, and early warning lookouts that protect the group from rivals, approaching law enforcement, or government agents. These new foot soldiers will also conduct reprisal violence against government collaborators.[128] Gang and insurgent cell leaders maintain a constant presence in the neighborhood, to serve as a visible symbol of control.

## NEW ORLEANS: A CASE STUDY ANALYSIS

For a number of years New Orleans, Louisiana, has ranked among the most violent cities in the United States. In fact, New Orleans has topped the list of United States cities with the highest murder rate on multiple occasions. A U.S. Justice Department, (DoJ) Bureau of Justice Assistance (BJA) study released in March 2011, analyzed New Orleans' crime data collected from 2009-2010. The BJA report revealed that New Orleans experienced a rate of fifty-two homicides per 100,000 residents, which, at the time of the study, was ten times the national average (figure 8). A comparative analysis of murder statistics reveals that New Orleans' homicide rate was nearly five times that of cities of comparable population size (250,000-499,999 residents).[129] For example, Orlando, Florida is comparable to New Orleans in population size and economic base, both cities rely on tourism as their main source of income. During reporting year 2009-2010, Orlando experienced fifty-four percent more total crimes, however, New Orleans' murder rate outpaced Orlando's by more than a four to one ratio.[130]

---

[128]Galula, *Counterinsurgency Warfare: Theory and Practice*, 43–57.

[129]Charles Wellford, Brenda J. Bond, and Sean Goodison, *Crime in New Orleans: Analyzing Crime Trends and New Orleans' Response to Crime*, Bureau Of Justice Assistance Crime Study (New Orleans, LA: Bureau of Justice Assistance, 15 March 2011), 4.

[130]Ibid.

Photo Removed Due to Copyright Restrictions

Figure 8. Murder Rate Comparison.

*Source:* Bureau Of Justice Assistance Crime Study. *Crime in New Orleans: Analyzing Crime Trends and New Orleans' Response to Crime.*

In a 2010 poll conducted by the Kaiser Foundation, citizens of New Orleans indicated that crime was the most serious problem facing the city.[131] With the probable exception of the mass relocation of citizens, citywide cleanup, and revitalization in the immediate aftermath of Hurricane Katrina, homicides and homicide reduction have been the most concerning social, political, and law enforcement issues plauging New Orleans' government, and its residents. Current Mayor Mitch Landrieu stated the following, "It remains my top priority as Mayor of New Orleans to end the cycle of violence on our streets."[132]

Homicides on the streets of New Orleans are not acts of random violence. Analysis of 200 homicide cases shows that homicides in New Orleans are purposeful, they overwhelmingly

---

[131]Ibid.

[132]Mayor Mitch Landrieu, *NOLA For Life*, Crime Reduction Strategy (New Orleans, LA: The City of New Orleans, May 2012).

have similar motive characteristics.[133] Over seventy-two percent of the sample cases reported three variables as the predominant incident motives. The most often reported motive variables include the following, as a single cause, or in some combination: drug related incidents (twenty-nine percent), revenge (twenty-four percent) and argument/conflict (nineteen percent).[134] The three primary motives attributed to most murders in New Orleans are closely correlated to gang activity.

The purposeful use of homicide in New Orleans is consistent with the process of gang violence noted earlier in this study. Gangs in New Orleans use homicide as a tool to protect their criminal enterprise and to control a specific territory. Although only one percent of the studied cases officially identified either the homicide victim, or offender as being gang affiliated, this is likely owning to the transient characteristics and loose organizational affiliation of New Orleans gangs.[135] New Orleans does in fact have criminal gangs operating within the city's neighborhoods. The point, that needs emphasis, is that they are not the traditionally structured gangs observed in other cities. "They are groups of individuals that identify themselves with the area in which they live and often create names for their groups. Sometimes these groups are as small as three to four individuals."[136]

Max Manwaring's three generations model is a useful guide for assessing and identifying a gang's structure and function. The type of gangs that are prevalent in New Orleans combine the

---

[133]Wellford, Bond, and Goodison, *Crime in New Orleans: Analyzing Crime Trends and New Orleans' Response to Crime,* 7.

[134]Ibid., 8.

[135]Ibid., 12.

[136]Ibid. Gangs in New Orleans do not have long historical ties, like those in some larger cities. The familiar large organized gang monikers such as Crips, Bloods, Gangster Disciples, and MS-13. While large gangs have some connections in the city, they are not as prevalent as are loosely affiliated first generation neighborhood gangs.

characteristics of first and second-generation gangs.[137] In general, gangs in New Orleans are loosely organized, the base of operations for their criminal enterprise rarely expands beyond the neighborhood where the gang developed and its members live. However, in some cases New Orleans gangs have evolved from a loose organization into a more structured hierarchy. Research indicates that this evolution into the realm of second-generation gang is necessary to manage an expanded criminal enterprise, primarily drug distribution.[138] Although there is no evidence to suggest that any gangs in New Orleans control a citywide area of operation, the gangs' use of violence for the purposes of coercion, control, and retaliation against rivals, does extend beyond the spatial boundaries of the respective neighborhood.

Detailed analysis of New Orleans' homicides indicates that victims and offenders overwhelmingly represent the young male, (16-35), demographic, most of whom have had prior formal contact with law enforcement. More than fifty percent of the offenders and the victims were males younger than twenty-seven years old at the time of incident. Furthermore, approximately fifty percent of the homicide victims and known offenders had no gainful employment listed in their case files. In addition to being young, male, and unemployed, in the aggregate, more than seventy-five percent of victims and offenders had at least one formal police contact prior to the homicide case.[139] The BJA's research data indicates that New Orleans homicide victims and offenders are products of disorganized social structures.

---

[137]Manwaring, "Street Gangs: The New Urban Insurgency."

[138]Ibid.

[139]Wellford, Bond, and Goodison, *Crime in New Orleans: Analyzing Crime Trends and New Orleans' Response to Crime*, 12. The source authors use the term—contacts rather than arrests, because they included offenses that did not lead to a formal arrest; the issue of importance is how many times an individual was in contact with law enforcement such that an official record of any kind was created. Violent offenses are the most common in offender histories, whereas drug offenses were most common in victims; among the known offenders, approximately 58

49

New Orleans is spatially divided into eight discrete districts. The city's eight districts are vastly different with respect to levels of educational attainment, family structure, employment and income level. Most of the violent crime in New Orleans is concentrated within the spatial area of four police districts (figure 9).[140] The first, fifth, sixth, and seventh districts in New Orleans, each, have significant concentrations of low wage earners, single parent households, and adults with less than a high school diploma.[141] Evidence reveals that the existing conditions in some districts are consistent with the social-economic indicators of socially disorganized neighborhoods, as described by Thrasher, Shaw, and McKay. Therefore, following the theoretical progression from social disorganization to gang formation, outlined earlier in this monograph, it is apparent that the patterns of interaction between the young men and the social environment in the first, fifth, sixth, and seventh districts of New Orleans amplify the conditions precedent to neighborhood gang development.[142] Sixth district is unique because the larger district area includes one of the most affluent neighborhoods in New Orleans. The Garden District is a high income, highly educated, and socially organized zone one neighborhood (government control). However, located just blocks away in sixth district is Central City, a notoriously high crime area in New Orleans that accounts for nearly all of sixth districts muder statistics.

---

percent had a drug offense, compared to more than 67 percent of victims. Finally, about the same proportion of offenders as victims had a prior firearms arrest (more than 41 percent of known offenders).

[140]Ibid. Data derived from the analysis of a sample size of 200 homicides committed in New Orleans between April 2009 and May 2010. Sixth district is included primarily because of the high density of murders concentrated in that districts Central City neighborhood.

[141]U.S. Census 2010 Summary File, "Central City Statistical Area," census and demographic data, *CommunityDataCenter.org*, December 20, 2012, http://www.gnocdc.org/NeighborhoodData/2/CentralCity/index.html (accessed January 18, 2014)

[142]Robert Axelrod and Michael D. Cohen, *Harnessing Complexity Organizational Implications of a Scientific Frontier* (New York: Basic Books, 2000), 63.

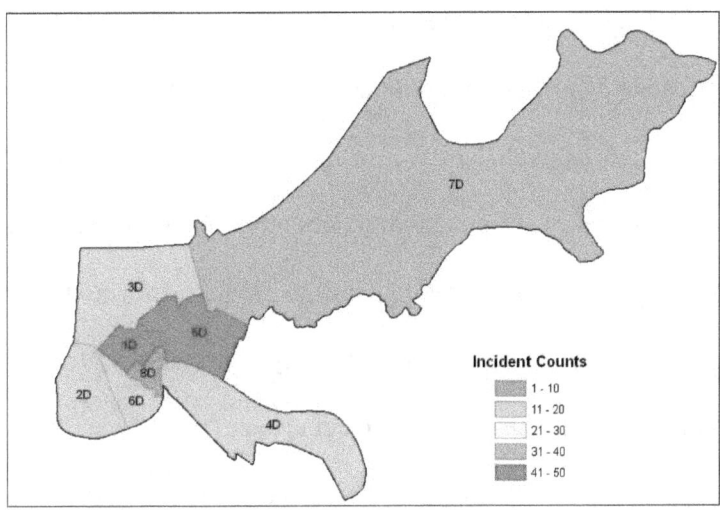

Figure 9. Homicides Incidents by District.

*Source:* Bureau of Justice Assistance Crime Study, *Crime in New Orleans: Analyzing Crime Trends and New Orleans' Response to Crime.*

The first, fifth, sixth, and seventh districts of New Orleans are not the only districts with the characteristics of socially disorganized neighborhoods, and gang violence is certainly unwelcomed by nearly all members of those communities. However, it is instructive to compare the density of murders, to the neighborhoods with high concentrations of unemployed, under educated, young males from single parent households. Given the current data, and using the zones of control model for analysis, first, fifth, sixth, and seventh districts in New Orleans each, separately, represent zone five, gang control.[143]

---

[143]Kalyvas, *The Logic Of Violence in Civil War.* Kalyvas uses zones to analyze the levels of insurgent and government control; the author of this monograph substitutes insurgent for gang in this instance.

The New Orleans Police Department (NOPD) assessed, in 2012, that a relatively well-defined collection of gangs and their members are responsible for most of the murders committed in New Orleans. The perpetrators of the crimes include approximately 600 gang members that make up thirty separate gangs operating in the New Orleans metropolitan area.[144] Although there are some well-organized gangs in the city, the gangs in New Orleans, primarily, are loosely organized groups affiliated with a particular neighborhood, city block, street corner or an area of the city known as a ward.[145] Neighborhood gangs in the first, fifth, sixth, and seventh districts, (zone of control five), account for a disproportinately high share of New Orleans' homicides.[146]

An examination of the federal indictment against "New Orleans' most dangerous criminal" Telly Hankton and his criminal network provides a vivid illustration of this research.[147] The network of family members, friends and neighborhood associates that self-organized in the mid-1990s into the criminal gang led by Telly Hankton, operated primarily in the Central City area of New Orleans. Central City is located in the sixth district of New Orleans, a zone five area plagued by indicators of social disorganization.

More than forty percent of Central City residents earn less than poverty wages, $1,250 per month. A high percentage of Central City families are single-parent households. According to

---

[144]Naomi Martin, Local News, NOLA.com, 8 November 2012, http://www.nola.com/crime/index.ssf/2012/11/mayor_mitch_landrieu_unveils_n.html (accessed 22 August 2013).

[145]Gangs in New Orleans are not challenging city law enforcement or rival gangs for control of a citywide crime enterprise; rather they primarily have very localized influence.

[146]Wellford, Bond, and Goodison, *Crime in New Orleans: Analyzing Crime Trends and New Orleans' Response to Crime*. Out of the 200 homicide cases reviewed by the BJA, first district accounted for forty-two (42) homicides, fifth district fifty (50) and seventh district thirty-three (33), the next highest murder victim total was sixth district twenty (20).

[147]Paul Murphy, "Background on Convicted Murderer Telly Hankton," *Wwltv.com*, 19 October 2012, http://www.wwltv.com/news/crime/Background-on-convicted-murderer-Telly-Hankton-174951071.html. (accessed February 4, 2014)

2010 census data, fifty-two percent, of Central City children under age eighteen live with their mother only. Approximately thirty percent of Central City residents over the age of twenty-five have achieved less than a high school equivalency education.[148] The concentration of socio-economic indicators in Central City are consistent with those of socially disorganized neighborhoods.

A federal racketeer influenced corrupt organization (RICO) indictment, named thirteen relatives and associates as members of the Hankton Central City gang.[149] Their criminal enterprise operated from within a four square block section of Central City, primarily headquartered out of the family's home.[150] Since the mid-1990s, the Hankton gang operated continuously in Central City without fear of denouncement because the group had deep-seated roots, familial ties and close neighborhood associations. Their connection to the neighborhood afforded the gang with the attitudinal and behavioral support of the population, which contributed to the gang having increased control of their territory, "the feds say family, friends, even his mother, helped the gang prosper."[151]

---

[148]U.S. Census 2010 Summary File, "Central City Statistical Area."

[149]U.S. Attorney Jim Letten, *Superseding Indictment for Violations of the Racketeer Influenced Corrupt Organization Act, The Violent Crime in Aid of Racketeering Act, The Federal Controlled Substances Act, The Federal Gun Control Act, Perjury, Money Laundering, Misprison of a Felony and Obstruction of Justice* (Louisiana: United States District Court, Eastern District of Louisiana, n.d.), 1.

[150]**Ibid.** The Central City area bordered by Jackson Avenue, St. Andrew Street, Simon Boliver Avenue and Oretha Castle Haley Boulevard is where Telly Hankton and several of his relatives lived.

[151]Brendan McCarthy and Paul Murphy, "Feds: Hankton Organization Was a Modern Day Crime Family," news website, *Wwltv.com*, 30 October 2012, http://www.wwltv.com/news/crime/Mother-of-convicted-murderer-Telly-Hankton-taken-into-custody-in-major-crime-roundup-174949311.html (accessed February 4, 2014)

Having the support of the population and control of the geographic territory increased the gang's sense of security. There was little chance that the government could infiltrate the Hankton network, to coerce a member to defect, or to convince the population to collaborate with law enforcement. The gang's sense of security within its environment reflects in the choice of a small operational cell structure (figure 5) to organize its functions and activities.

The Hankton federal indictment alleges the gang constituted a criminal enterprise whose function and purpose included, "enriching members of the enterprise through distribution of controlled substances, preserving and protecting the power and territory of the enterprise, and keeping witnesses in fear of the enterprise and its members, through violence and the threat of violence and intimidation."[152]

Since 1996, Hankton's gang "allegedly moved hundreds of kilos of cocaine, some heroin, marijuana and more. And in order to run that drug business, authorities say, they shot, killed and intimidated people, including some of their own."[153]

The Hankton gang developed and operated an extensive network of violent criminal activity within one of New Orleans' disorganized neighborhoods for over fifteen years. However, in October of 2011, after a member of the Hankton family allegedly murdered a prosecutorial witness' brother, the violence had surpassed the theoretical violence threshold (figure 3), "that killing provoked outrage in the community. Mayor Mitch Landrieu and others portrayed Telly Hankton as Public Enemy Number One, the most dangerous man in New Orleans."[154] In a public statement, New Orleans Mayor Mitch Landrieu pledged to "go after" the Hankton criminal gang

---

[152]Letten, *Superseding Indictment for Violations of the Racketeer Influenced Corrupt Organization Act, 3.*

[153]McCarthy and Murphy, "Feds: Hankton Organization Was a Modern Day Crime Family."

[154]Ibid.

including family members and associates. The mayor's statement signaled that the government, law enforcement and citizens would unify in effort to regain control of the Central City neighborhood that Hankton's gang dominated.[155]

## RECOMMENDATIONS

Much like counterinsurgency operations, efforts to counter gangs and reduce gang violence in urban neighborhoods are highly complex. Counterinsurgency and counter-gang programs are essentially competitions for control, popular support, and legitimacy within a territory. The government's capacity to protect its citizens and provide for their welfare determines the extent of their success in countering insurgents and gangs.[156] The *Clear-Hold-Build* approach, popularized by twentieth century counterinsurgency theorists, and used successfully as the theoretical basis for the 2007 shift in the Iraq War strategy, (commonly referred to as the *"surge")*, provides a comprehensive methodology to help New Orleans reduce its gang-related murders and establish control in the city's most violent neighborhoods.[157]

An operational approach adhering to the clear-hold-build model should initially focus on high-priority areas under insurgent control, zone five. The object is to surge security forces into the area clearing it of violent offenders and subversive elements creating an environment that is physically secure, controlled by the government, and where the population feels safe.[158] Immediately after removing the violent offenders, the government's forces should seek to hold

---

[155]John Simerman, "Mayor Mitch Landrieu 'Sends a Message' to Telly Hankton and His Family at Site of Killing," *Times Picayune*, 18 October 2011, nola.com online edition, http://www.nola.com/crime/index.ssf/2011/10/new_orleans_mayor_ sends_a_mess.html (accessed February 5, 2014)

[156]Department of the Army, FM 3-24, 1-28.

[157]David H. Ucko, *The New Counterinsurgency Era: Transforming the U.S. Military for Modern Wars* (Washington, DC: Georgetown University Press, 2009), 74.

[158]Department of the Army, FM 3-24, 5-18.

the area by establishing security stations, and increasing the frequency of patrols in the recently cleared area. Clearing and holding the area provides the time and space required for the government to strengthen its relationships in the community and develop programs to address the root causes of insurgency in the area.[159]

In order to address the immediate problem of reducing high murder rates, while simultaneously resolving the systemic issues leading to gang formation and high homicide rates, New Orleans should employ a multi-disciplinary approach unifying the efforts of law enforcement agencies, government institutions, and community organizations.

## Current Conditions

New Orleans has a murder rate ten times the national average, and approximately five times higher than cities of comparable size. The high rates of homicide in New Orleans are generally concentrated in four areas first, fifth, sixth and seventh districts. Although community relations are improving, there is a historic and persistently high lack of trust between the communities most plagued by violent crime and the law enforcement agency sworn to protect them, the New Orleans Police Department (NOPD). The offenders and victims of homicides primarily are members of distinct demographic, young males with prior drug and firearm related criminal records.

Gangs in New Orleans are not formally structured, hierarchical gangs as seen in larger cities, Chicago and Los Angeles for example. The lack of structure in New Orleans gangs is what makes them more problematic. Gang research indicates that large gangs with formal structures, rules and hierarchies replicate civil institutions by providing social services and security to the

---

[159]Department of the Army, FM 3-24.

communities they control.[160] It is also important to recognize that, structured gangs offer control mechanisms for intra-and inter-gang conflict resolution. In New Orleans, however, this is not the case.

New Orleans neighborhood street gangs do not have a structured hierarchy, and for obvious reasons they do not refer disputes over profits, personal injury, or territorial claims to legitimate civil authorities; "street justice" is the first resort for dispute resolution. It is counterintuitive that small ill-structured neighborhood gangs produce far more deadly results than large formal gangs can.[161] However, the complex interaction occurring in disorganized neighborhoods between New Orleans gangs, their rivals, and the local populations produce disproportionately high effects, an excessive homicide rate.

### Desired End State

Mayor Landrieu's vision, as outlined in the NOLA for Life Strategy, is to transform New Orleans into a city where, "[y]outh and families flourishing in safe and healthy neighborhoods, with access to high quality educational, economic, and cultural opportunities that allow everyone to become self-reliant, self-sufficient and creative human beings capable of giving back to the world."[162] The Mayor intends to accomplish his vision by, "work[ing] with community and agency partners to develop and implement a comprehensive strategy that reduces murders in the City of New Orleans by employing targeted prevention, intervention, enforcement and rehabilitation initiatives."[163]

---

[160]Knox, *An Introduction to Gangs*, 291.

[161]Gharajedagi, *Systems Thinking Managing Chaos and Complexity*, 49.

[162]Landrieu, *NOLA for Life*, 7.

[163]Ibid.

The recommended operational approach, figure 10, proposes four lines of effort designed to help New Orleans achieve control in its contested neighborhoods and implement programs to eliminate the sources of instability in the most troubled areas of the city. The supported objectives are specific goals associated with each line of effort intended to guide progress towards realization of the desired conditions and ultimately achieving Mayor Landrieu's desired end state for New Orleans. The supporting narrative describes recommended operational approach within the clear-hold-build model.

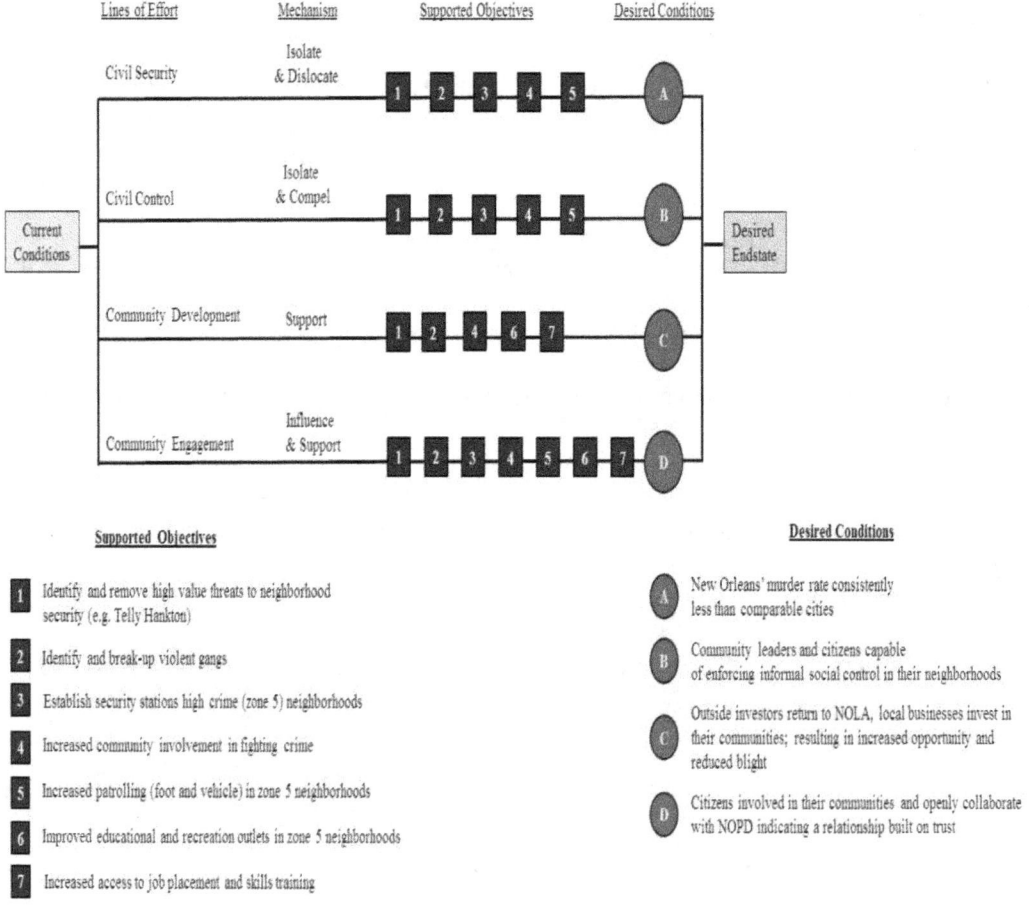

Figure 10. The Operational Approach

*Source:* Created by author.

## Clear

In order to "end the cycle of violence" and "murder epidemic" present in some neighborhoods, establishing civil security and control are the priority efforts.[164] An effective way to combat the gang violence is to intensify targeting and inter-agency "strike" operations.[165] Strike operations are a vital element of counterinsurgency operations because security forces aggressively and continuously target insurgent leaders and individuals of high intelligence value. Successful strike operations typically benefit counterinsurgents in a number of ways: 1) removes an insurgent leader for the area, 2) generates intelligence for future strike operations, 3) denies insurgent's freedom of movement, and 4) disrupts their base of support.

To be effective, strike operations targeting New Orleans gangs would require a combined effort by local law enforcement supported by state and federal agencies specifically in the areas of intelligence gathering and analysis tools. The New Orleans Multi-Agency Gang Unit (MAG) established in 2012 is an ideal organization to operate in the clear phase of this approach. Mayor Landrieu described the MAG's value in a 2012 press conference, "whereas homicides in the past have typically been investigated as isolated incidents, prosecutors in the gang unit will work alongside detectives to develop evidence of group ties and patterns of violence. The goal is to get indictments of entire groups on charges such as conspiracy and racketeering, which carry hefty jail time".[166]

---

[164]Ibid., 3.

[165]Department of the Army, FM 3-24.2, 3-23.

[166]Martin, NOLA.com.

Strike operations supported by accurate intelligence serve to remove violent criminals from the neighborhoods and for a short time disrupts the gang. However, because of their aggressive and, sometimes, intrusive nature, strike operations may undermine the already fragile relationship between the neighborhood population and the police.

## Hold

A major component in the shift in the OIF strategy was to establish forward bases in the contested areas, this allowed security forces to stay in touch and develop relationships with the people they were meant to protect.[167] Forward operating bases and, smaller, combat outposts are critical for establishing control and intelligence gathering within the contested population.[168] The author recommends renovating existing structures within the zone five districts (first, fifth, sixth, and seventh) and establishing them as forward operating bases staffed with a consistent cadre of law enforcement professionals assigned to the targeted community. Manning at the forward operating base should consist of a multi-functional team of patrolmen, investigators, emergency medical treatment, and a representative from the district attorney's office. The forward bases' physical structure should include two holding cells to detain suspects for short durations, not more than twenty-four hours, while awaiting transfer to central lock-up. The forward operating base would serve as the command and control element for smaller community outposts; in addition the forward bases would help in closing the divide between the neighborhoods and City Hall.

Small combat outposts should be deployed into historical neighborhood gang hot-spots, the Hankton gang's neighborhood for example. The physical structure of the outpost should

---

[167]Department of the Army, FM 3-24, 1-27.

[168]Department of the Army, FM 3-24.2, 6-9.

consist of a building or house positioned near a key area of gang activity. The outpost would be manned contiuously, with members from the districts forward operating base on rotating shifts. To ensure accurate analysis and timely response to tips and actionable intelligence, the forward deployed teams should be equipped with all necessary communications and data collection tools, including a Crimestoppers phone line and handheld biometric toolsets.[169] New Orleans crime data illustrates patterns of homicides. Implementation of pattern analysis tools to analyze the data would reveal enough information to determine homicide hotspots specific enough to target for surveillance or patrol.

Civil control is all about people. Successfully gaining control requires the targeted communities to participate and buy-in to the efforts to control their neighborhoods. Government and law enforcement agencies provide formal control, and organized communities provide informal control. Cooperation and collaboration between the local authorities and the citizens are prerequisites to building safe and secure neighborhoods.[170] The Civil Control line of effort emphasizes continuity in police-community relations and civil engagement. Continuity allows time to build the necessary relationships, community contacts and confidential informants required to increase intelligence gathering. Without developing relationships and gaining the trust

---

[169]"Crimestoppers Is a Local New Orleans Initiative. It Is a Telephone Hotline That Allows Witnesses to Crime or Citizens," n.d. Crimestoppers is a local New Orleans initiative. It is a Telephone hotline that allows witnesses to crime or citizens that have information to anonymously share with police. Handheld biometrics equipment is frequently used by U.S. military patrols. The systems allow the users to quickly compare a suspect's biometric data, (fingerprints for example) against an electronic database of biometrics collected at previous crime scenes.

[170]Warner, Beck, and Ohmer, "Linking Informal Social Control and Restorative Justice," 357.

of the people, the NOPD will not collect the information needed to gain control of the zone five districts.[171]

## Build

The root of New Orleans' high murder lays within its concentration of disorganized neighborhoods, and is exaserbated by the distrust and lack of collaboration between the government and the population. Since 2012 New Orleans has greatly increased its civic engangement efforts and has instituted a series of reforms within the police department. The city's approach has started to bridge the divide between the NOPD and the community, particularly in zone five areas. However, there is work to be done beyond civic engagement.

The build phase of the approach focuses on reinforcing the gains made in local security and the gaining control of the neighborhoods. The build phase addresses building popular support, and building a viable community. It is imperative to design programs that provide immediate benefit to the community combined with longer term investments and development programs that address the root causes of violent crimes. The cadre stationed at the district forward bases should have access to resources allowing them to nominate immediate impact projects to supplement community engagement efforts.

The community development and community engagement lines of effort are collaborative and will require unity of effort from the community, the government, and business sponsors. Commitment to changing the culture of violence plauging some New Orleans communities will require long term investment in programs dedicated to improving education, employment, and the physical conditions for New Orleans' most disorganized neighborhoods. It is also important to

---

[171]Department of the Army, FM 3-24, 3-1.

expose those most at risk to homicide (young males) to opportunities outside of their immediate four block by four block neighborhood.

## CONCLUSION

The similarities between insurgents and street gangs described in this research, supports the hypothesis that counterinsurgency methods are applicable to fighting New Orleans' neighborhood gangs. U.S. Army counterinsurgency (COIN) doctrine provides numerous methods of fighting against insurgencies. Many of the methods outlined in COIN doctrinal manuals provide feasible options to assist New Orleans' government and law enforcement in the fight against neighborhood street gangs.

The United States military plays a prominent role in counterinsurgency operations. However, success in COIN requires unity of effort and a comprehensive approach from all instruments of national power and multiple agencies, government and non-government. Many counterinsurgency theorists have concluded that a COIN operation should win the support of the contested population by addressing needs other than security.[172] Using the clear-hold-build model guided by clear lines of effort provide a comprehensive approach to winning the population's support, and ecouraging defection of former insurgent fighters and supporters.

In 2012 Mayor Landrieu and the City of New Orleans launched NOLA for Life, a comprehensive murder reduction strategy. Mayor Landrieu's strategy consists of a multifaceted approach, highlighting three strategic goals.[173] The first goal, as outlined in the Group Violence Reduction Strategy, is to "develop, implement and support multi-disciplinary and data-driven initiatives that address the following four pillars: prevention, intervention, enforcement and

---

[172]Ibid., 2–1.

[173]Landrieu, *NOLA for Life*.

rehabilitation. The mayor's strategy also aims to, "facilitate effective interagency communication and information sharing." Finally, the violence reduction strategy will, "promote civic engagement to support the reduction of violence."[174] The Group Violence Reduction Strategy is designed to target and defeat the estimated five percent of the population that are responsible for the homicides.[175] The NOLA for Life Strategy is similar in scope to the whole of government, population-centric approach applied in United States COIN doctrine.

The comprehensive murder reduction strategy involves multiple law enforcement and civic agencies, from the local state and federal level. All working in unified effort to solve the underlying problems leading to the growth and development of street gangs in New Orleans' disorganized neighborhoods. However, in addition to New Orleans' ongoing police reforms, civic engagment campaign, and community revitilization, the author recommends an operational approach that includes four lines of effort, (1) civil security, (2) civil control, (3) community development, and (4) community engagement The recommended approach will enhance the city's current violent crime reduction strategy and help New Orleans regain control of its neighborhood streets.

---

[174]Ibid.

[175]Martin, NOLA.com.

## BIBLIOGRAPHY

Axelrod, Robert, and Michael D. Cohen. *Harnessing Complexity Organizational Implications of a Scientific Frontier*. New York: Basic Books, 2000.

Bynam, Daniel. *Understanding Proto-Insurgencies*. RAND Counterinsurgency Study Paper 3. Santa Monica, CA: RAND: National Defense Research Institute, 2007.

Department of the Army. Field Manual (FM) 3-24, *Counterinsurgency*. Washington DC: Government Printing Office, 2006.

_____. Field Manual (FM) 3.24.2, *Tactics in Counterinsurgency*. Washington DC: Government Printing Office, 2009.

Department of Justice. " Organized Crime and Gang Section." About Violent Gangs. http://www.justice.gov/criminal/ocgs/gangs/ (accessed 4 January 2014).

Dolman, Everett Carl. *Pure Strategy: Power and Principle in the Space and Information Age*. New York: Frank Cass, 2005.

Evans, Edward, and James Spies. "Insurgency in the Hood: Understanding Insurgencies Through Urban Gangs." Master's thesis, Naval Postgraduate School, 2006.

Farah, Douglas. "Central America's Northern Triangle: A Time for Turmoil and Transitions." *PRISM* 4, no. 3 (2013). 88-109.

Federal Bureau of Investigation. *National Gang Threat Assessment: Emerging Trends*. Federal Bureau of Investigation Report. http://www.fbi.gov/stats-services/publications/2011-national-gang-threat-assessment/2011-national-gang-threat-assessment#CurrentGang (accessed 5 February 2014).

Finn, Peter and Jerry Murphy Healy. *Preventing Gang and Drug Related Witness Intimidation*. U.S. Department of Justice Report. Washington DC: National Institute of Justice, November 1996. http://babel.hathitrust.org/cgi/pt?id= purl.32754066627625;page=root;view=image;size=100;seq=3;num=i (accessed February, 4, 2014)

Freeman, Michael, and Hy Rothstein. "Gangs and Guerillas: Ideas from Counterinsurgency and Counterterrorism." Defense analysis report. Naval Post- Graduate School, Monterrey, CA, March 2011.

Galula, David. *Counterinsurgency Warfare: Theory and Practice*. St Petersburg, FL: Hailer Publishing, 2005.

Gerth, H. H., and C. Wright Mills. "Politics as Vocation." In *Max Weber: Essays in Sociology*, 77–128. New York: Oxford University Press, 1946. http://www.sscnet. ucla.edu/polisci/ethos/Weber-vocation.pdf. (accessed December 29, 2013).

Gharajedagi, Jamshid. *Systems Thinking Managing Chaos and Complexity*. 2nd ed. New York: Elsevier Inc, 2006.

Hatch, Mary Jo, and Ann L. Cunliffe. *Organization Theory*. 2nd ed. New York: Oxford University Press, 2006.

Howell, James C. "Youth Gangs: An Overview." *Juvenile Justice Bulletin* (August 1998): 1–15.

Joes, Anthony James. *The History and Politics of Counter Insurgency*. Lexington, KY: The University Press of Kentucky, 2004.

Kalyvas, Stathis N. *The Logic of Violence in Civil War*. New York: Cambridge University Press, 2006.

Kitson, Frank. *Low Intensity Operations: Subversion, Insurgency, and Peacekeeping*. St. Petersburg, FL: Hailer Publishing, 2006.

Knox, Dr. George W., *An Introduction to Gangs*. 6th ed. Chicago, IL: New Chicago School Press, 2006.

Landrieu, Mayor Mitch. *NOLA for Life*. Crime Reduction Strategy. New Orleans, LA: The City of New Orleans, May 2012.

Letten, U.S. Attorney Jim. *Superseding Indictment for Violations of the Racketeer Influenced Corrupt Organization Act, The Violent Crime in Aid of Racketeering Act, The Federal Controlled Substances Act, The Federal Gun Control Act, Perjury, Money Laundering, Misprison of a Felony and Obstruction of Justice*. Louisiana: United States District Court, Eastern District of Louisiana, n.d.

Manwaring, Max G. "Street Gangs: The New Urban Insurgency." Carlisle, PA: U.S. Army War College, 2005.

Martin, Naomi. NOLA.com, 8 November 2012. http://www.nola.com/crime/ index.ssf/2012/11/mayor_mitch_landrieu_unveils_n.html (accessed 22 Aug 2013).

McCarthy, Brendan, and Paul Murphy. "Feds: Hankton Organization Was a Modern Day Crime Family." Wwltv.com, 30 October 2012. http://www.wwltv.com/news/ crime/Mother-of-convicted-murderer-Telly-Hankton-taken-into-custody-in-major-crime-roundup-174949311.html (accessed February 4, 2014)

McCuen, John J. *The Art of Counter-Revolutionary War*. Harrisburg, PA: Stackpole Books, 1965.

Moghaddam, Fathali M. "The Staircase to Terrorism." *American Psychologist* 60, no. 2 (March 2005): 161–69.

Molnar, Andrew, Jerry M. Tinker, and John D. LeNoir. *Human Factors Considerations of Undergrounds in Insurgencies*. U.S. Army Research, Center for Research In Social Systems The American University, Washington, DC December, 1966.

Murphy, Paul. "Background on Convicted Murderer Telly Hankton." Wwltv.com, 19 October 2012. http://www.wwltv.com/news/crime/Background-on-convicted-murderer-Telly-Hankton-174951071.html (accessed February 4, 2014)

National Gang Intelligence Center. *2011 National Gang Threat Assessment – Emerging Trends*. FBI Report, http://www.fbi.gov/stats-services/publications/2011-national-gang-threat-assessment/2011-national-gang-threat-assessment#Executive (accessed February 4, 2014)

Sahadi, Jeanne. "What Gang of Six Plan Would Do." *CNN Money*, 19 January 2011. http://money.cnn.com/2011/07/19/news/economy/gang_of_six_budget/ (accessed December 29, 2013)

Senge, Peter M. *The Fifth Discipline: The Art and Practice of the Learning Organization*. New York: Doubleday, 2006.

Simerman, John. "Mayor Mitch Landrieu 'Sends a Message' to Telly Hankton and His Family at Site of Killing." *Times Picayune*. 18 October 2011, nola.com online. http://www.nola.com/crime/index.ssf/2011/10/new_orleans_mayor_sends_a_mess.html (accessed December 29, 2013)

_____. "New Orleans Taliban Gang Targeted in State." *The Advocate: New Orleans Edition*, 18 August 2013. http://theadvocate.com/news/neworleans/6785061-148/new-orleans-taliban-gang-targeted (accessed December 29, 2013)

"Social Disorganization Theory and Rural Communities." Government Website. *OJJDP Bulletin*, May 2003. https://www.ncjrs.gov/html/ojjdp/193591/page1.html (accessed December 29, 2013)

Spergel, Irving A. *The Youth Gang Problem: A Community Approach*. New York: Oxford University Press, 1995.

Sullivan, John P. "Future Conflict: Gangs and Intelligence." *Small Wars Journal*, 2009. smallwarsjournal.com (accessed February, 4, 2013)

Thrasher, Fredric M. *The Gang: A Study of 1,313 Gangs in Chicago*. Chicago, IL: University of Chicago Press, 1927.

Trinquier, Roger. *Modern Warfare: A French View of Counterinsurgency*. London: Pall Mall Press, 1961.

Tse-Tung, Mao. *Selected Military Writings of Mao Tse-Tung*. Ft. Leavenworth, KS: Combat Studies Institute, 1985.

Ucko, David H. *The New Counterinsurgency Era: Transforming the U.S. Military for Modern Wars*. Washington, DC: Georgetown University Press, 2009.

U.S. Census 2010 Summary File. "Central City Statistical Area." Census and demographic data. CommunityDataCenter.org, 20 December 2012. http://www.gnocdc.org/NeighborhoodData/2/CentralCity/index.html (accessed January 18, 2014)

Warner, Barbara D., Elizabeth Beck, and Mary L. Ohmer. "Linking Informal Social Control and Restorative Justice: Moving Social Disorganization Theory beyond Community Policing." *Contemporary Justice Review* 13, no. 4 (December 2010): 355–69.

Wellford, Charles, Brenda J. Bond, and Sean Goodison. *Crime in New Orleans: Analyzing Crime Trends and New Orleans' Response to Crime*. New Orleans, LA: Bureau of Justice Assistance Crime Study, 15 March 2011.

Wood, Jane, and Emma Alleyne. "Street Gang Theory and Research: Where Are We Now and Where Do We Go from Here?" *Aggression and Violent Behavior*, no. 15 (2010): 101–11.

Zabel, Lt Col Sarah E. "Military Strategy of Global Jihad." Student Paper, United States Army War College, Carlisle, PA 2007.